Dear Customer

Welcome to the Exotic World of Sugam Paneer.

You have made the right choice for the perfect authentic taste of a delicacy and a delight that has tickled many a palate, all over since time immemorial.

This book introduces you to the world of elegant cooking of Sugam Paneer. It gives you a wide variety of choice in cooking, all from the International Award winner, cooking expert, Mrs Nita Mehta.

You have the best! Now go ahead and try out these recipes. Please remember your feedback is very important to us. Hence, do not hesitate in writing your views on our products, recipes and your entire experience in being associated with us.

Ukay Khoa Manufacturing Ltd.

Unit E2, Whiteacres, Whetstone,

Leicestershire,

LE8 6ZG

Tel: 0116 284 9930

Fax: 0116 284 9931

E-mail: info@sugampaneer.com

Website: www.sugampaneer.com

Sugam Paneer **IS** Sugam Paneer

There is no other paneer like Sugam Paneer and Sugam Paneer is not like any other paneer.

Nita Mehta's
Exotic Cooking with

PANEER

Nita Mehta

M.Sc. (Food and Nutrition), Gold Medalist

SNAB
Publishers Pvt. Ltd.

Nita Mehta's
Exotic Cooking with

PANEER

© Copyright 2005 **SNAB** Publishers Pvt Ltd

First Hardbound Edition 2005

ISBN 81-7869-103-5

Food Styling & Photography: **SNAB**

Layout and laser typesetting:

National Information Technology Academy
3A/3, Asaf Ali Road
New Delhi-110002 (India)

Published by:

SNAB
Publishers Pvt Ltd

Editorial and Marketing office:
E-159, Greater Kailash-II, New Delhi-110048 (India)

Printed at:
BRIJBASI ART PRESS LTD.

Ukay Khoa Manufacturing Ltd.
Unit E2, Whiteacres, Whetstone,
Leicestershire, LE8 6ZG
E-mail: info@sugampaneer.com
Website: www.sugampaneer.com

Price: UK £ 14.99

INTRODUCTION

*J*n every home, Sugam Paneer is the queen of dishes. A rich source of protein, it is very versatile and easy to use. Sugam Paneer is used with many vegetables to create nutritious and well balanced meals. Besides being used for Indian delights, it can be very deliciously used in Continental, Chinese and Thai dishes. This book offers *Green Thai Sugam Paneer Curry, Stuffed Cheese Steaks* and many other wonderful dishes. In the recipe *Iman Binaldey*, Sugam Paneer is very successfully combined with chickpeas (kabuli chaanas). The dish is then baked to produce a Continental delight. Tofu is substituted with the easily available Sugam Paneer in noodles for the Chinese food lovers. In the Indian section there are innovative dishes like *Pepper Sugam Paneer Chettinad* and *Manzil-e-Sugam Paneer.*

There are snacks which can be served as starters before a meal and many tea time snacks for the evenings. The evergreen *Sugam Paneer Tikka* and other tandoori snacks are very simple to make once you follow the recipes step by step. The pictures of the steps will make the job very simple. A few snacky meals like *Chilli Sugam Paneer Dosa* are new creations for the evenings.

With this book besides you, surprise your friends with creations they will not anticipate. Use this book for a variety of new Sugam Paneer dishes for your parties and family get together. Enjoy!

Nita Mehta

Contents

Starters   11

Tips you must go through...

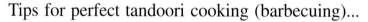

Tandoori   30

Tips for perfect tandoori cooking (barbecuing)...

Tea Time & Snacky Meals   46

Indian Meal Time Dishes
Dry & Masala   67

Indian Meal Time Dishes
Gravies & Curries   84

Chinese & Thai   125

Continental   139

Glossary of Names/ Terms   159

Herbs & Spices

	ENGLISH NAME		HINDI NAME
1	Sesame Seeds	1	Til
2	Mustard Seeds	2	Rai, Sarson
3	Melon Seeds	3	Magaz
4	Coriander Seeds	4	Saboot dhania
5	Coriander Seeds, Ground	5	Dhania powder
6	Mango Powder	6	Amchoor
7	Red Chilli Powder	7	Lal Mirch
8	Cumin Seeds, White	8	Jeera
9	Carom Seeds	9	Ajwain
10	Fennel	10	Saunf
11	Cumin Seeds, Black	11	Shah Jeera
12	Garam Masala - A Spice Blend	12	Garam Masala
13	Asafoetida	13	Hing
14	Saffron	14	Kesar
15	Fenugreek Seeds, Dried	15	Kasoori methi
16	Fenugreek Seeds	16	Methi dana
17	Pomegranate Seeds, Dried	17	Anardana
18	Nigella Seeds	18	Kalaunji
19	Turmeric	19	Haldi
20	Cloves	20	Laung
21	Nutmeg	21	Jaiphal
22	Peppercorns	22	Saboot kali mirch
23 24	Cardamom Pods	23 24	Illaichi
25	Mace	25	Javitri
26	Cinnamon	26	Dalchini
27	Fresh Green Chillies	27	Hari mirch
28	Red Peppercorns, Dried	28	Sukhi lal mirch
29	Ginger	29	Adrak
30	Garlic	30	Lahsun
31	Coriander, Fresh	31	Hara dhania
32	Bay Leaves	32	Tej patta
33	Curry Leaves	33	Kari patta
34	Mint	34	Poodina

INTERNATIONAL CONVERSION GUIDE

These are not exact equivalents; they've been rounded-off to make measuring easier.

WEIGHTS & MEASURES

METRIC	IMPERIAL
15 g	½ oz
30 g	1 oz
60 g	2 oz
90 g	3 oz
125 g	4 oz (¼ lb)
155 g	5 oz
185 g	6 oz
220 g	7 oz
250 g	8 oz (½ lb)
280 g	9 oz
315 g	10 oz
345 g	11 oz
375 g	12 oz (¾ lb)
410 g	13 oz
440 g	14 oz
470 g	15 oz
500 g	16 oz (1 lb)
750 g	24 oz (1½ lb)
1 kg	30 oz (2 lb)

LIQUID MEASURES

METRIC	IMPERIAL
30 ml	1 fluid oz
60 ml	2 fluid oz
100 ml	3 fluid oz
125 ml	4 fluid oz
150 ml	5 fluid oz (¼ pint/1 gill)
190 ml	6 fluid oz
250 ml	8 fluid oz
300 ml	10 fluid oz (½ pint)
500 ml	16 fluid oz
600 ml	20 fluid oz (1 pint)
1000 ml	1¾ pints

CUPS & SPOON MEASURES

METRIC	IMPERIAL
1 ml	¼ tsp
2 ml	½ tsp
5 ml	1 tsp
15 ml	1 tbsp
60 ml	¼ cup
125 ml	½ cup
250 ml	1 cup

HELPFUL MEASURES

METRIC	IMPERIAL
3 mm	1/8 in
6 mm	¼ in
1 cm	½ in
2 cm	¾ in
2.5 cm	1 in
5 cm	2 in
6 cm	2½ in
8 cm	3 in
10 cm	4 in
13 cm	5 in
15 cm	6 in
18 cm	7 in
20 cm	8 in
23 cm	9 in
25 cm	10 in
28 cm	11 in
30 cm	12 in (1ft)

HOW TO MEASURE

When using the graduated metric measuring cups, it is important to shake the dry ingredients loosely into the required cup. Do not tap the cup on the table, or pack the ingredients into the cup unless otherwise directed. Level top of cup with a knife. When using graduated metric measuring spoons, level top of spoon with a knife. When measuring liquids in the jug, place jug on a flat surface, check for accuracy at eye level.

OVEN TEMPERATURE

These oven temperatures are only a guide; lower degree of heat are given. Always check the manufacturer's manual.

	°C (Celsius)	°F (Fahrenheit)	Gas Mark
Very low	120	250	1
Low	150	300	2
Moderately low	160	325	3
Moderate	180	350	4
Moderately high	190	375	5
High	200	400	6
Very high	230	450	7

STARTERS
Tips you must go through...

- The most delicious snack in the world can fail to tempt if it is presented in an unbecoming manner! A greasy or too oily snack is no more appetizing, so make it a habit to remove the fried snack from oil on a tissue or a paper napkin to absorb the excess oil.

- A few crisp leaves of lettuce or a sprig of mint or coriander placed at the edge of the serving platter makes the snack irresistible! Make the green leaves crisp by putting them in a bowl of cold water and keeping them in the fridge for 3-4 hours or even overnight. Some cucumber slices or tomato wedges placed along with the greens, beautify it further.

- A teaspoon of til (sesame seeds) or khus-khus (poppy seeds) or ajwain (carom seeds), added to coating mixture or bread crumbs makes the snack interesting.

- For getting a crisp coating on cutlets or rolls, dip prepared snack in a thin batter of maida and water and then roll in bread crumbs. Fry till well browned.

- In the absence of bread crumbs, a mixture of ¼ cup maida and ½ cup suji may be used to get a crisp coating.

- If your cutlets fall apart, quickly tear 1-2 slices of bread and grind in a mixer to get fresh bread crumbs. Add it to the cutlet mixture for binding.

- To make crisp potato chips, soak them in cold water for 1 hour. Drain. Wipe dry and sprinkle some maida (plain flour) on them before frying.

- Never start frying in smoking hot oil as it will turn the snack black. Never fry in cold oil also as the snack may fall apart or it may soak a lot of oil.

- For deep frying any snack, add small quantities to the oil at one time. This maintains the oil's temperature. If too many pieces are added together, the oil turns cold and a lot of oil is then absorbed by the snack.

- After deep frying, let the oil cool down. Add a little quantity of fresh oil to the used oil before reusing. This prevents the oil from discolouring.

Chilli Sugam Paneer

Picture on facing page   Serves 12

INGREDIENTS

250 gms/8 oz Sugam Paneer- cut into 1" squares
1 large capsicum - cut into ½" pieces
1 tomato - pulp removed & cut into ½" pieces
4-5 flakes garlic - crushed
1 tbsp vinegar
1½ tbsp soya sauce
3 tbsp tomato ketchup
½ tbsp chilli sauce
½ tsp salt and ½ tsp pepper, or to taste
3 tbsp oil

THICK COATING BATTER
¼ cup plain flour (maida)
½ tsp salt, ¼ pepper
¼ cup water

METHOD

1 Cut Sugam Paneer into 1" squares, capsicum cut into ½" pieces.

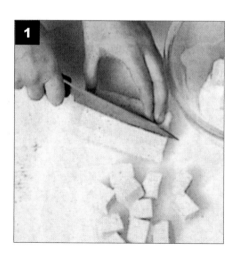

2 Mix all ingredients of the coating batter.

3 Dip the Sugam Paneer in maida batter and deep fry till golden brown. Keep aside.

4 Heat 3 tbsp oil. Reduce heat. Add garlic. Let it turn light brown.

5 Remove from heat. Add vinegar, soya sauce, tomato ketchup, chilli sauce, salt and pepper. Return to heat and cook the sauces on low heat for ½ minute.

6 Add capsicum, Sugam Paneer and tomato pieces. Mix well. Stir for 1-2 minutes. Remove from heat.

7 Thread a capsicum, then a Sugam Paneer and lastly a tomato piece on each tooth pick. Serve.

Achaari Sugam Paneer Cigars

Picture on facing page   *Makes 28 pieces*

INGREDIENTS

DOUGH
1 cup plain flour (maida), 1 tbsp oil
½ tsp salt, a pinch of baking powder

FILLING
2 cups mashed Sugam Paneer (200-250 gm/ 8oz)
¼ cup chopped coriander
1 onion - very finely chopped
1 green chilli - deseeded & chopped
2 tbsp oil, 1 tsp fennel (saunf)
½ tsp cumin seeds (jeera)
½ tsp mustard seeds (rai)
¼ tsp turmeric (haldi), ½ tsp garam masala
¾ tsp salt or to taste, ½ tsp red chilli powder
1 tbsp lemon juice or to taste
2 tbsp tomato ketchup

COATING
1 tbsp sesame seeds (til), 6 tbsp dry bread
crumbs, a pinch of orange food colour

BATTER (MIX TOGETHER)
¼ cup (plain flour) maida
¾ cup water, ¼ tsp salt & ¼ tsp pepper

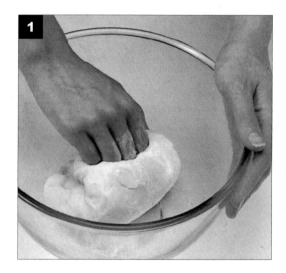

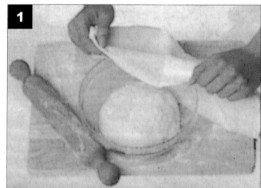

METHOD

1   Mix maida, oil, salt and baking powder. Add enough water and knead well to make a firm dough. Cover and keep the dough aside for 20-30 minutes.

2   For filling, heat oil. Add saunf, jeera & rai. Wait for 1 minute. Add onions, stir till soft. Add haldi, garam masala, salt and chilli powder. Add Sugam Paneer and cook on moderate heat till dry. Add coriander and green chillies. Add lemon juice & cook for 1 minute. Remove from heat & keep aside.

3 Make very thin chappatis, each as big as the chakla (8"-9" diameter) on low heat on a tawa, keeping it white. Remove from tawa. Keep soft in a casserole.

4 Cut each chappati into 4 pieces to get 4 triangular pieces. On each piece put 1½ tbsp of filling, 1" away from the pointed end and roll up to cover filling.

5 Fold the right and left side a little to enclose the filling and holding the folded sides firmly, roll up to get a cigar shaped roll. Seal the end with a little tomato ketchup. Keep it on a flat surface with the joint side down.

6 Mix bread crumbs with til and food colour in a bowl. Spread only 2 tbsp on a plate. Dip each roll in maida batter and then press over bread crumbs. Keep aside, covered with cling film till serving firm.

7 To serve, deep fry till crisp. Serve plain or with any chutney.

Lachhedar Sugam Paneer Crisps

An extremely crisp snack coated with thin vermicelli (seviyaan).

Picture on facing page   *Makes 12- 14*

INGREDIENTS

2½ cups grated Sugam Paneer (250 gms/8 oz)
3 slices bread - churned in a mixer to get
fresh bread crumbs
½ cup chopped coriander
¾ tsp chaat masala
½ tsp roasted cumin powder (bhuna jeera)
¾ tsp salt, ½ tsp pepper

FILLING
¼ cup yellow split peas (channa dal) - soaked
for 2 hours & ground coarsely without water
in a mixer
1 onion - chopped finely
1 tsp finely chopped ginger
1 tbsp cashews (kaju) - chopped
2 tbsp raisins (kishmish) - chopped, 1 tbsp oil
¼ tsp turmeric (haldi), ½ tsp salt
¼ tsp red chilli powder
¼ tsp amchoor, ½ tsp garam masala

TO COAT
½ cup very thin vermicelli (seviyaan) -
roughly broken into small pieces by hand

METHOD

1   Strain dal and roughly grind in a mixer to a coarse thick paste. Do not grind too much and make it thin and smooth.

2   Heat oil. Add onion, ginger, cashews and raisins. Cook till onions turn light golden.

3   Add ground dal, haldi, salt, red chilli powder, amchoor and garam masala. Stir for 1-2 minutes. Remove from heat and keep filling aside.

4   Mix grated Sugam Paneer with coriander, chaat masala, fresh bread crumbs, bhuna jeera, salt and pepper.

5 With a ball of the Sugam Paneer mixture, make a 2" long oval roll. Flatten it to get a slight depression in the centre. Place 1 tsp of the filling in it along the length. Pick up the sides to cover the filling, such that the filling is completely covered on all sides with the Sugam Paneer mixture. Shape to give a neat roll with slightly flattened ends.

6 Break seviyaan into 1-1½" small pieces. Spread on a plate. Take 1 cup of water separately in a shallow flat bowl (katori). Dip the roll in the water for a second and then immediately roll it over the seviyaan. All the sides should be completely covered with seviyaan.

7 Keep aside to set for 15 minutes. Deep fry 2-3 pieces at a time. Serve with poodina chutney.

Jalapeno & Cheese Croquettes

Jalapenos are pronounced as hale- pea- noz, 'j' being pronounced as 'h'. Quick and delicious croquettes, these taste even better with the cheesy dip given below. Must give it a try.

Picture on facing page   *Makes 8 croquettes*

INGREDIENTS

90 gm/3 oz Sugam Paneer - grated (1 cup)
125 gms/4 oz mozzarella cheese- grated
(1¼ cups)
½ tsp black pepper powder
½ salt, or to taste, oil for frying
1 slice of bread - churned in a mixer to get
fresh bread crumbs
3 jalapenos - chopped finely

COATING
½ cup plain flour (maida)
1 cup dry bread crumbs - to coat

METHOD

1 Tear bread into pieces and churn in a mixer to get fresh crumbs.

2 Mix grated Sugam Paneer, cheese, jalapenos, pepper, salt and bread crumbs.

3 Divide the mixture into 8 equal portions Shape each portion into a ball.

4 Shape each ball into a roll, about 2" long. Flatten the sides of the roll, by pressing the sides of the roll against a flat surface. Keep aside.

5 Spread maida and bread crumbs in separate flat plates. Take 1 cup of water separately in a shallow flat bowl. Roll croquettes over maida. Then dip the croquette in the water for a second and then immediately roll it over the dry bread crumbs. All the sides should be completely covered with bread crumbs.

6 Heat oil in a kadhai and fry 2 croquettes at a time till golden brown. Serve with cheesy yogurt dip given below.

Cheesy Yogurt Dip

INGREDIENTS

½ cup yogurt - hang for ½ hour in a muslin cloth
¼ tsp oregano
3 tbsp cheese spread, 1 tbsp milk
¼ tsp salt, ¼ tsp pepper
¼ tsp red chilli flakes

METHOD

1 Mix all together till smooth. Serve with croquettes or any chips, etc.

Mewa Rolls

Extremely soft and delicious rolls. Make extra as they are usually eaten more than expected, especially at parties.

Picture on facing page   *Makes 20-22*

INGREDIENTS

a few toothpicks, optional
1 tbsp magaz (melon seeds) & 1 tbsp sun-flower seeds (chironji) or 2 tbsp chopped almonds (badam) - dry roast on a tawa
2 cups grated Sugam Paneer (200 gms/6 oz)
½ cup dry bread crumbs, see note
1 tbsp cornflour
½ tsp garam masala, ¾ tsp salt
¼ tsp red chilli powder, a pinch of amchoor

PASTE
¼ tsp jaiphal (nutmeg), ¼ tsp mace (javetri)
10 kaju (cashewnuts), 8 almonds (badam)
5 raisins (kishmish)
5-6 whole pistachio (pistas)
2 green chillies, ¼ cup green coriander
1" piece ginger, 6-8 flakes garlic

METHOD

1 Roast magaz and chironji or almonds on a hot tawa. Cool.

2 Grind all ingredients given under paste in a mixer with 3 tbsp water till smooth.

3 Mix grated Sugam Paneer, roasted chironji, magaz, bread crumbs, cornflour, garam masala, salt, red chilli powder, amchoor and the prepared paste. Mix well.

4 Take a lemon sized ball of the mixture. Make a small roll of 1½" length. Flatten it from the sides. Pass a toothpick through the rolls, if using.

5 Heat oil in a kadhai. Deep fry the 2-3 rolls at a time along with the toothpicks till golden brown. Drain on napkins. Serve hot.

Note: Store dry bread crumbs in an air tight container in the refrigerator. Dry crumbs are available in the market. To make them at home: Tear 3 bread slices into small pieces and spread in a microproof plate/ dish. Micro high for 2 minutes. Mix with hands to change sides and again micro high for 1 minute. Remove from microwave and let it stand for 15 minutes or till dry. Grind in a mixer.

Vegetable Seekh

Picture on facing page   *Makes 15*

INGREDIENTS

½ **cup mashed** Sugam Paneer
1 cup whole red lentils (saboot masoor ki dal)
1" piece ginger, 8-10 flakes garlic
1 green chilli - chopped
1 tsp cumin seeds (jeera)
2 cloves (laung) & seeds of 2 green cardamom
(chhoti illaichi) - powdered
3 tbsp cornflour
1¼ tsp salt or to taste, 1 tsp garam masala
1 tsp red chilli powder, ¼ tsp amchoor
½ piece of a bread - churn in a mixer to get
fresh bread crumbs
2½ tsp lemon juice, 3-4 tbsp oil
3 tbsp capsicum - chopped
3 tbsp onion- chopped
2 tbsp tomato (without pulp)- finely chopped

METHOD

1 Soak saboot masoor dal for 2 hours. Strain.

2 Grind dal, ginger, garlic, green chilli and jeera to a thick smooth paste using the minimum amount of water. Keep dal paste aside.

3 Heat 3 tbsp oil in a heavy bottomed kadhai. Add dal. Stir-fry for 4-5 minutes on low heat till dal is dry and does not stick to the bottom of the kadhai. Remove from heat.

4 Mix powdered laung and illaichi, cornflour, Sugam Paneer, salt, garam masala, red chilli powder, amchoor and bread crumbs with the dal. Add lemon juice, 2 tbsp of chopped capsicum, 2 tbsp of chopped onion, 1 tbsp of chopped tomato. Reserve the rest. Mix well. Make balls out of the mixture. Keep aside.

5 Take a ball of dal paste & make a 2" long kebab.

6 Take a skewer and push it from one end of the kebab to the other end, along the length of the kebab.

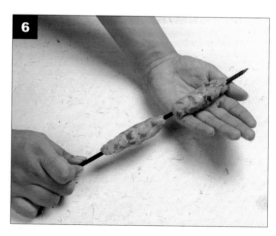

7 Stick remaining chopped onion, capsicum and tomatoes (without pulp) on kebab by pressing vegetables with the palm on to the kebab.

8 Gently pull out the skewer from the kebab.

9 Shallow fry the seekh in medium hot oil on a pan to a light brown colour. Serve hot with chutney.

For more info, visit: www.sugampaneer.com

Amritsari Sugam Paneer

A snack resembling our all time favourite Sugam Paneer pakoras.

Picture on facing page   *Serves 4*

INGREDIENTS

250 gms/8 oz (½ lb) Sugam Paneer
12-15 flakes of garlic &
1½" piece of ginger - crushed to a paste or
2 tbsp ginger-garlic paste
½ tsp carom seeds (ajwain)
a few drops of orange food colour
½ tsp salt, ½ tsp pepper & red chilli powder
5-6 tbsp (gram flour) besan or more
oil for frying
ready-made chat masala to sprinkle on
Sugam Paneer

METHOD

1 Cut Sugam Paneer into thin long fingers.

2 Mix ginger-garlic paste, ajwain, food colour, salt, pepper & red chilli powder in a shallow bowl.

3 Add the Sugam Paneer fingers, mix gently so that all the sides of Sugam Paneer gets coated with the spices. Keep Sugam Paneer aside till serving time.

4 At serving time, heat oil in a kadhai on medium heat.

5 Spread besan in a flat plate. Pick up one piece of Sugam Paneer at a time and coat with the besan spread in the plate. Coat on all the sides. Repeat for all the Sugam Paneer pieces. Add more besan if required.

6 Deep fry till crisp and golden brown. Drain on paper napkins. Serve generously sprinkled with chaat masala.

Is the oil ready for frying?

Put a tiny piece of bread in hot oil. If the oil sizzles and the bread turns golden within 30 seconds, and comes to the surface, go ahead and fry the paneer. Extra hot oil will turn the bread dark brown. If the oil is not hot enough, the bread will quietly remain at the bottom and it will absorb too much oil during browning.

Crispy Pakoras!

For crispy pakoras, make batter with ice cold water and fry them twice. Half fry them before and fry them again at serving time. However paneer pakoras should be fried only once because frying them a second time makes them chewy. Also, adding a little oil to the batter makes crisp pakoras.

Curry Patta Toasties

Picture on facing page   Serves 4

INGREDIENTS

75 gm/3 oz **Sugam Paneer** - crumbled or mashed roughly (¾ cup), 2 tbsp semolina (suji) ½ tsp salt, or to taste, ¼ tsp pepper, or to taste ½ onion - very finely chopped ½ tomato - cut into half, deseeded and chopped finely 2 tbsp curry leaves, 3 bread slices - toasted ¼ - ½ tsp small brown mustard seeds (rai) 3 tsp oil to shallow fry

METHOD

1 Mix the suji, salt and pepper with the Sugam Paneer using your fingers.

2 Add the onion, tomato and curry leaves.

3 Spread this mixture carefully on the toasted bread slices, keeping the edges neat.

Note: This recipe will work best using a minimum quantity of oil for frying.

4 Sprinkle some rai over the mixture, pressing down carefully with your finger tips.

5 Heat 1 tsp oil in a pan. Add a slice of bread with the topping side down.

6 Cook until it turns golden brown and crisp. Add a little more oil for the next slice if required. Cut into 8 triangular pieces and serve hot.

Sugam Paneer Mango Submarine : Recipe on page 47 ➤

Kalyani Sugam Paneer

Beautiful rounds of Sugam Paneer filled with a delicious filling. The leftover Sugam Paneer could be used for various recipes like Lachhedar Sugam Paneer Crisps, Mewa Seekh in Gravy or for delicious Achaari Sugam Paneer Cigars, etc. ...so there is no wastage. Go ahead!

Picture on facing page   *Makes 8-10 pieces*

INGREDIENTS

500 gm/1 lb Sugam Paneer (take a big block or a single piece weighing 500 gms)

FILLING
1 potato - boiled and grated finely
1 tbsp very finely chopped coriander
½ tsp salt or to taste
½ tsp roasted cumin powder (bhuna jeera)
½ tsp garam masala, ¼ tsp red chilli powder
1½ tbsp very finely chopped mixed nuts
(almonds, pistachios, raisins etc.)
8-10 whole almonds (badaam)

COATING
¼ cup plain flour (maida), ½ tsp salt
½ tsp pepper, ½ tsp chaat masala

METHOD

1 Cut Sugam Paneer into 1" thick slices lengthwise. Cut each slice into rounds of about 1½" diameter with a small sharp lid or a cover of any small round container. This way you get small, thick Sugam Paneer rounds.

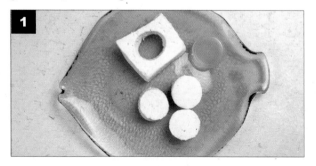

2 In each round, with the help of a scooper or knife make a shallow hole, about ½" deep in the centre, leaving ¼" wall all around. Go a little deep and not too wide. Leave the bottom intact to fill the filling.

3 Sprinkle some chaat masala on hollow Sugam Paneer circles.

4 For filling, boil a potato, peel and grate very finely.

5 Mix all the ingredients of the filling with the potatoes. Check seasonings, mix well.

6 Make very tiny balls of the potato mixture that would fit into the scooped out hollow of Sugam Paneer. Place the ball over the Sugam Paneer hole and press gently to flatten a little. Let the potato topping cover some of the sides of the Sugam Paneer hole, making the edges of the hole neat.

7 Press one whole piece of badam on the filling in the rounds. Press gently so that it sticks in the centre.

8 Mix all the coating ingredients and spread in large flat plate. Coat the Sugam Paneer circles in it, turning to coat all sides of the Sugam Paneer and the filling.

9 Heat oil in a kadhai and deep fry the circles till golden brown. Drain on paper napkins. Serve hot.

TANDOORI

- Never over grill Sugam Paneer. It turns hard on doing so. Also, you can marinate it well in advance but it should be put in a preheated oven just about 20-30 minutes before serving time, so that it can be served straight from the oven. Reheating the Sugam Paneer can sometimes make it hard. If reheating becomes necessary, brush the tikka nicely with some melted butter before putting it in the oven. Also cover it with some foil so that the direct heat does not affect it and make it hard.

- Tandoori food should be barbecued on the grill rack or wire rack (*jaali*) of the oven and not on the oven tray. When the food is put on the tray, the liquid that drips keeps collecting around the food. This does not let the food get crisp on the outside. When it is on the wire rack, the liquid drips down. These drippings can be collected on a tray covered with aluminium foil and placed under the rack.

- Cut the pieces of Sugam Paneer according to the space in between the wires of the grill. If the distance between the wires of the rack is too wide, and there is a chance of your piece slipping, then cover the wire rack with a well greased **aluminium foil**.

- The size of tikkas should not be **too small**. After getting cooked they shrink. A very small piece after getting cooked can turn hard.

- While skewering or placing pieces of Sugam Paneer, the pieces should be arranged such that there is atleast **1" gap** between them so that each piece can get it's own space and heat all around to get cooked properly.

Some Accompaniments to Tandoori Food...

1. Dahi Poodina Chutney:

Hang 1½ cups yogurt for 15 minutes in a muslin cloth.
Grind ½ cup coriander, ½ cup mint, 2 green chillies, ½ onion and 2 flakes garlic with a little water to a paste. Beat the hung yogurt well till smooth. Add prepared green paste, 1 tsp oil, pinch of kala namak, ¼ tsp roasted cumin powder (bhuna jeera) and salt to taste. Mix, serve.

2. Hot Chilli Garlic Chutney:

4-5 dry red chillies - deseeded and soaked in ¼ cup water, 6 flakes garlic, 1 tsp coriander seeds (saboot dhania), 1 tsp cumin (jeera), 1 tbsp oil, ½ tsp salt, 1 tsp sugar, 3 tbsp vinegar, ½ tsp soya sauce. For the chutney, grind soaked chillies along with the water, garlic, dhania, jeera, oil and sugar and vinegar to a paste. Add soya sauce. Serve.

Achaari Sugam Paneer Tikka

Yellow, pickle flavoured masala Sugam Paneer tikka.

Makes 10-12

Picture on page 32

INGREDIENTS

400 gms/12 oz Sugam Paneer - cut into
1½" rectangles of ¾-1" thickness
2 tsp ginger-garlic paste
1 tbsp cornflour
1 cup yogurt - hang in a muslin cloth for ½ hour
½ tsp haldi (turmeric) powder
1 tsp dried mango powder (amchoor)
1 tsp coriander powder (dhania)
½ tsp garam masala
1 tsp salt or to taste
½ tsp sugar
1 onion - chopped finely
2 green chillies - chopped
2 tbsp oil
some chaat masala to sprinkle

BASTING (POURING ON THE TIKKAS)
some melted butter/oil for basting the tikkas

ACHAARI MASALA
1 tbsp fennel (saunf)
½ tsp sarson (mustard seeds)
a pinch of fenugreek seeds (methi daana)
½ tsp onion seeds (kalonji)
½ tsp cumin seeds (jeera)

METHOD

1 Hang yogurt in a muslin cloth for 15 minutes.

2 Collect all the seeds of achaari masala together in a small bowl.

3 Heat oil. Add collected seeds together to the hot oil. Let saunf change colour.

4 Add onions and chopped green chillies. Cook till onions turn golden brown.

5 Reduce heat. Add haldi, amchoor, dhania powder, garam masala, salt and sugar. Mix. Remove from heat. Let it cool down.

8 Add the Sugam Paneer pieces to the yogurt. Marinate till serving time.

6 Beat yogurt till smooth.

9 At serving time, rub oil generously over the grill of the oven or wire rack of a gas tandoor. Place Sugam Paneer on the greased wire rack or grill of the oven.

10 Heat an oven to 180°C/350°F or a gas tandoor on moderate heat. Grill Sugam Paneer for 15 minutes. Spoon some oil or melted butter on the Sugam Paneer pieces in the oven or tandoor and grill further for 5 minutes. Serve hot sprinkled with chaat masala.

7 Add the onion masala, garlic-ginger paste, and cornflour to the well beaten curd.

For more info, visit: www.sugampaneer.com

33

Haryali Tikka

Picture on facing page   Serves 6

INGREDIENTS

**400 gm/12 oz Sugam Paneer - cut into
1½" long pieces, 1" thick
4 tbsp gram flour (besan)
1 tsp salt
4 tbsp oil**

**GRIND TO A FINE PASTE (CHUTNEY)
1 cup fresh green coriander (green dhania)
2 tsp fennel (saunf)
1" piece ginger
5-6 flakes garlic
½ tsp salt, 4 tbsp lemon juice**

METHOD

1 Cut Sugam Paneer into 1½" long pieces, 1" thick.

2 Grind together dhania, saunf, ginger, garlic, salt and lemon juice to a fine paste.

3 Slit the Sugam Paneer pieces almost till the end and keep aside.

4 Divide the chutney into 2 parts.

5 With one part of the chutney, stuff some chutney in the slits of all the Sugam Paneer pieces. Keep the stuffed Sugam Paneer aside.

6 Mix together the left over chutney with besan, salt and oil. Rub this all over the stuffed Sugam Paneer pieces.

8 Heat an oven to 180°C/350°F or a gas tandoor on moderate heat. Grill Sugam Paneer for 15 minutes. Spoon some drops of oil on the Sugam Paneer pieces in the oven or tandoor and grill further for 5-10 minutes. Serve hot.

7 Rub oil generously over the grill of the oven or wire rack of a gas tandoor. Place Sugam Paneer on the greased wire rack or grill of the oven.

Note: To cook the tikkas in the oven, place a drip tray under the wire rack on which the tikkas are placed, to collect the drippings.

Sugam Paneer Kakori

Very soft and delicious vegetarian seekh kebabs.

Picture on facing page   *Makes 15*

INGREDIENTS

1 cup crumbled or roughly mashed Sugam Paneer (100 gm/4 oz)
2 potatoes (medium) - boiled & mashed
2 cups (250 gm/8 oz) yam (jimikand) - chopped and boiled
½ cup cashewnuts (kaju) - ground
2 tsp ginger- garlic paste
1 onion - very finely chopped
2 green chillies - very finely chopped
2 tbsp green coriander - very finely chopped
1 tsp cumin roasted (bhuna jeera)
1½ tsp salt, 1 tsp red chilli powder
¼ tsp amchoor
3 slices of bread - torn into pieces and churned in a mixer to get fresh crumbs
a pinch of tandoori red food colour

INGREDIENTS FOR LATER USE
2 tbsp melted butter or oil, chaat masala

METHOD

1 Cook chopped yam with 1 cup water and ½ tsp salt till soft. Mash it with a karchhi or a potato masher on low heat till dry. Remove from heat. Keep aside.

2 Mix Sugam Paneer, mashed potatoes, jimikand and all other ingredients, making a slightly stiff paste.

3 Rub oil generously on the wire rack or grill of the oven or gas tandoor. Oil and wipe the skewers.

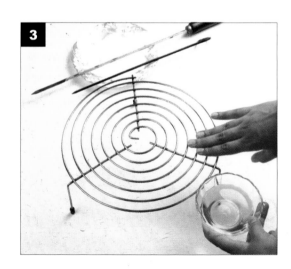

4 Press kebab mixture into finger-shaped kebabs on the skewers. Brush them with oil or rub oil on the palms & shape them with oiled hands. Cook in a tandoor or grill for about 8-10 minutes or till golden brown. Pour some melted butter on the kebabs to baste them. Turn them only when they are almost done otherwise they tend to break. Spoon some oil on the other side also and grill for 5 minutes or till done.

5 Sprinkle tandoori or chaat masala on the kebabs and serve with onion rings sprinkled with lemon juice and chaat masala and lemon wedges.

Note: If you do not wish to grill the kebabs, pull out from skewers and shallow fry in 1 tbsp oil in a pan, turning sides till browned evenly.

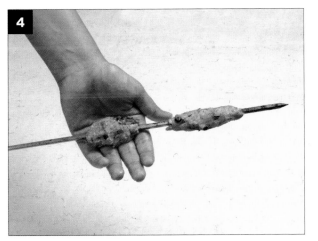

Tikka Reshmi

Tikkas are finished with cream to give them a silky soft taste.

Picture on facing page   Serves 4-5

INGREDIENTS

**250 gms/8 oz Sugam Paneer - cut into
1½" cubes (8 pieces)
2 capsicums - cut into 1" pieces
2 onions - cut into 1" pieces
3 tbsp gram flour (besan), 2 tbsp yogurt
1 tsp salt, ¼ tsp red chilli powder
½ tsp garam masala, ¼ tsp pepper
1 tbsp lemon juice, 2 tbsp oil**

**GRIND TOGETHER TO A PASTE
1½" piece ginger, 3-4 flakes garlic
1 tsp cumin seeds (jeera)
seeds of 2 chhoti illaichi
2 tbsp chopped coriander, 2-3 green chillies**

**OTHER INGREDIENTS
4-5 tbsp thick cream or fresh malai - beaten
well till smooth**

METHOD

1 Grind garlic, ginger, jeera, chhoti illaichi, coriander and green chillies to a paste.

2 Add besan, yogurt, salt, chilli powder, garam masala, pepper and lemon juice to the paste.

3 Cut Sugam Paneer into 1½" cubes. Put the paste in a big bowl and add the Sugam Paneer pieces and mix well so as to coat the paste nicely on all the pieces. Add the onion and capsicum pieces also and mix lightly. Keep aside till serving time.

4 At serving time, rub oil generously over the grill of the oven or wire rack of a gas tandoor. Place Sugam Paneer on the greased wire rack or grill of the oven.

5 Heat an oven to 180°C/350°F or a gas tandoor on moderate heat. Grill Sugam Paneer for 15 minutes. Spoon some oil or melted butter on the Sugam Paneer pieces in the oven or tandoor and grill further for 5 minutes.

38

6 Heat malai or cream in a clean kadhai on very low heat, to make it just warm. Do not let it turn into ghee by keeping on the heat for a longer time.

7 Add the grilled Sugam Paneer and vegetable pieces. Toss gently.

8 Serve on a bed of onion rings sprinkled with some chat masala.

Tandoori Makai Mirch

Good as a side dish for a meal. Sugam Paneer cubes and corn mixed with mozzarella cheese. On cooking the cheese melts, binding all together.

Picture on facing page　　　　　*Serves 4*

INGREDIENTS

4 medium size capsicums or bell peppers

MARINADE
2 tbsp lemon juice, 1 tsp ginger paste
½ tsp garlic paste, 1 tbsp oil, ¾ tsp salt

STUFFING
100 gm/4 oz Sugam Paneer - cut into ¼" pieces
½ cup grated mozzarella cheese
½ cup corn kernels - tinned or freshly boiled
1 tbsp green coriander - chopped
¼ tsp hing (asafoetida)
1 tsp jeera (cumin seeds)
½ tsp mustard seeds (sarson)
1 small onion - cut into half and then into rings, to get shredded onion
1 tbsp chopped cashews (kaju)
8-10 kishmish (raisins)
½ tsp red chilli powder, ¾ tsp salt
½ tsp garam masala, ¼ tsp amchoor

BASTING
2 tbsp oil or melted butter

METHOD

1. Cut a thin slice from the top (stem end) of each capsicum. Scoop out the center with the help of a knife. Mix all the ingredients of the marinade and rub liberally on the inside of the capsicums. Cover with caps and leave aside for ½ hour.

2. Take a heavy bottom kadhai and heat 2 tbsp oil. Put in the hing, jeera, and sarson. Wait till jeera turns golden.

3. Add onions and cook till golden brown. Add cashews and kishmish. Stir. Add red chilli powder, salt, garam masala and amchoor.

4. Add corn and cook for 1 minute. Add Sugam Paneer and mix well. Remove from heat. Add coriander and mozzarella cheese. Mix. Keep filling aside.

5. Stuff the capsicums with this filling. They should be stuffed well but not to bursting point. Rub oil on the outside of the stuffed capsicums. Cover with the caps and secure them with wooden toothpicks.

5

6 Oil and wipe the skewers. Skewer the capsicums. Small onions or pieces of potatoes can be used in-between to prevent them from slipping. Put the skewers into the gas tandoor or grill and cook for 10 minutes or till they turn blackish at some places. Turn 1-2 times in-between to grill evenly. Serve.

Note: Capsicums can be placed on the wire-rack or grill rubbed with some oil, if you don't have skewers. It is then not necessary to fasten them with tooth picks.

Sugam Paneer Tikka

Sugam Paneer Tikka

Serves 4   *Picture on opposite page*

INGREDIENTS

300 gm/10 oz Sugam Paneer - cut into
1½" squares of 1" thickness
1 large capsicum - deseeded and cut into
1" pieces (12 pieces)
1 onion - cut into 4 pieces and then separated

MARINADE
½ cup yogurt- hang in a muslin cloth for 15 min
3 tbsp thick malai or thick cream
a few drops of orange food colour or a pinch of
turmeric (haldi)
1½ tbsp oil, 1 tbsp cornflour
½ tsp amchoor, ½ tsp kala namak
¾ tsp salt, or to taste, 1 tbsp tandoori masala

GRIND TOGETHER
1" piece ginger, 5-6 flakes garlic
2 dried, whole red chillies - soaked in
water for 10 minutes and drained

METHOD

1 Hang yogurt in a muslin cloth for 15 minutes.

2 Drain soaked red chillies. Grind ginger, garlic and red chillies to a paste.

3 To the ginger-garlic-chilli paste, add hung yogurt, cream or malai, food colour or haldi, 1½ tbsp oil, 1 tbsp cornflour, amchoor, kala namak, salt, tandoori masala and Sugam Paneer. Mix well.

4 Brush the wire rack (grill) of the oven generously with oil.

5 Arrange Sugam Paneer on a greased wire rack of the oven or on the skewers. After all the Sugam Paneer pieces are done, put the capsicum & onions - both together in the left over marinade and mix well to coat the vegetables with the marinade. Leave the vegetables in the bowl itself.

6 At the time of serving, put the Sugam Paneer pieces placed on the wire rack in the hot oven at about 180°C/350°F. Grill till almost done, for about 15 minutes. Grill the Sugam Paneer till it gets dry and starts getting crisp. Sprinkle some oil on the Sugam Paneer pieces. Now remove the vegetables from the bowl and put them also in the oven on the sides of the Sugam Paneer. Grill everything together for another 5 min. The vegetables should not be grilled for too long.

7 Remove from the oven. Serve immediately (really hot), sprinkled with some lemon juice and chaat masala.

Tandoori Chaat

Picture on facing page   *Serves 4*

INGREDIENTS

**200 gm/6 oz Sugam Paneer - cut into
1" square pieces
2 small onions - each cut into 4 pieces
2 tomatoes - each cut into 4 pieces and
pulp removed
2 capsicums - deseed and cut into 1½" pieces
(preferably 1 green & 1 red capsicum)
4 fresh pineapple slices - each cut into
4 pieces (see note)
1 tsp garam masala, 2 tbsp lemon juice
1 tbsp tandoori masala or barbecue masala
2 tbsp oil, 1 tsp salt, or to taste
1½ tsp chaat masala**

METHOD

1 Cut Sugam Paneer into 1" square pieces and
  cut capsicum into 1½" pieces.

2 Cut each onion and tomato into 4
  pieces. Mix all the vegetables,
pineapple and Sugam Paneer in a bowl.

3 Sprinkle all the ingredients on them.
  Mix well.

4 Grease the grill or wire rack of the oven or tandoor and first place the Sugam Paneer, pineapple and onions only on the grill rack. Grill at 180°C/350°F for about 15 minutes, till the edges start to change colour.

5 After the Sugam Paneer is almost done, put the capsicum and tomatoes also on the wire rack with it. Grill for 10 minutes.

6 Remove from the oven straight to the serving plate. Sprinkle some chaat masala and lemon juice, if you like.

Note: If tinned pineapple is being used, grill it in the second batch with capsicum and tomatoes since it is already soft.

TEA TIME &
SNACKY MEALS

Sugam Paneer Mango Submarine

These are not served hot like the usual footlongs. An Ideal low calorie snack for summers.

Serves 6   *Picture on page 27*

INGREDIENTS

**1 long French bread or garlic bread - cut
lengthwise to get 2 thin, long pieces
2 tbsp butter - softened, 2 tbsp oil
2 tbsp sweet mango chutney
1 cucumber (kheera) - cut into round slices
without peeling
2 firm tomatoes - cut into slices
few mint (poodina) leaves to garnish - dipped
in chilled water**

SPRINKLE ON SUGAM PANEER
400 gm/12 oz Sugam Paneer **- cut into ¼" thick
round slices with a cookie cutter
¼ tsp turmeric (haldi)
½ tsp chilli powder, ½ tsp salt
1 tsp chaat masala powder**

METHOD

1 Spread butter on the cut surface of both the pieces of bread, as well as a little on the sides. Place the breads in the oven at 200°C/400°F on a wire rack for 7-8 minutes till crisp and light brown on the cut surface. Keep aside.

2 Cut Sugam Paneer into ¼" thick slices and then cut the slices into round pieces with a cookie cutter. (See picture on page 28, step 1).

3 Sprinkle Sugam Paneer on both sides with some chilli powder, salt, haldi & chaat masala.

4 At serving time, heat 2 tbsp oil in a non stick pan. Saute Sugam Paneer pieces on both sides in 2 tbsp oil till slightly toasted to a nice yellowish-brown colour.

5 To assemble the submarine, apply 1 tbsp mango chutney on each piece of bread.

6 Sprinkle some chaat masala on the kheera and tomato pieces. Sprinkle some chat masala on the Sugam Paneer also.

7 Place a piece of Sugam Paneer, then kheera, then tomato and keep repeating all three in the same sequence so as to cover the loaf. Keep Sugam Paneer, kheera and tomato, slightly overlapping. Insert fresh mint leaves in between the vegetables, so that they show. Serve.

47

Chargrilled Caprika Pizza

This quick home made pizza of an unusual shape has a smoky flavour of roasted coloured bell peppers (capsicum). Do not wash the bell peppers after roasting or you will lose flavour, so wash before you roast them.

Picture on facing page   *Makes 3*

INGREDIENTS

THIN CRUSTY HOME MADE PIZZA BASE
¼ cup lukewarm water, ½ tsp sugar
2 tsp heaped dried yeast
1 teacup milk, 1½ tbsp oil, 1 tsp salt, 1 tsp sugar
300 gms/10 oz (3 packed cups) maida (plain flour)

TOPPING
100 gms/4 oz Sugam Paneer - grated finely (1 cup)
1 large green capsicum - cut into half & deseeded
1 large red capsicum - cut into half & deseeded
1 large yellow capsicum - cut into half & deseeded
2- 3 big mushrooms, optional
1 onion - cut into half and sliced to get semi circles
salt & oregano or pepper to taste, 1 tbsp oil
2 tbsp fresh parsley leaves - chopped finely or
1 tsp dry parsley
150 gm/5 oz grated mozzarella
cheese (1½ cups)
3 tbsp melted butter or olive oil

METHOD

1 Mix warm water and sugar in a deep, small bowl. Check that the water is lukewarm. Add yeast. Mix the yeast gently. Cover the bowl and leave it in a warm place till the granules of the yeast disappear and it becomes frothy. (10-15 min). (If it does not swell, discard it).

2 Mix milk, oil, salt and sugar in a pan. Keep aside. When the yeast becomes frothy, heat this milk mixture to make it lukewarm. Add the ready yeast mix to the luke warm milk mixture. Add this yeast and milk mixture to the maida and knead well to make a smooth dough.

3 Grease a big polythene bag, brush the dough with a little oil and put it in the polythene. Keep it covered in a warm place to swell for 1 hour or till it is double in size.

4 Now punch it down to its original size, brush with oil and keep it back in the polythene bag for another 15 minutes or till it swells again.

5 Make 3 balls. Spread a 10" square aluminium foil on a kitchen platform. Grease it with some oil. Flatten a ball of the dough on it using the fingers to a thin rectangular-oval pizza of about 10"x7" size. Prick each base with a fork. Brush pizza base with olive oil or any oil. Keep aside.

6 Wash and rub oil on the skin of the capsicums and mushrooms. Put them under the grill, skin side up till the skin is evenly charred with black spots. Remove from grill. Leave covered for 5-10 minutes. Do not wash even if there are some black patches left. (They taste and look good!). Chop into 1" pieces.

7 Sprinkle some grated cheese and Sugam Paneer over the base. Sprinkle parsley. Arrange roasted capsicums, mushrooms and onions. Sprinkle salt and oregano. Top with more grated cheese.

8 Drizzle some olive oil. Place the pizza with the aluminium foil on the wire rack of the oven (not tray) and bake at 180°C (350°F) for 15 minutes until golden and crisp.

For more info, visit: www.sugampaneer.com

Moong Dal Chillahs with Sugam Paneer

Picture on facing page   *Serves 4*

INGREDIENTS

1 cup split green gram (moong dal)
½ tsp salt
½ tsp red chilli powder
1½ tbsp finely chopped coriander
150-200 gms/6 oz Sugam Paneer - cut into
3" long fingers
2 tbsp oil
½ tsp salt, ½ tsp garam masala
½ tsp red chilli powder
1 tbsp chopped coriander

METHOD

1 Soak dal for 3-4 hours only. Do not soak for a longer period.

2 Strain. Grind with 1 cup water to a smooth batter. Add about ½ cup water to get a pouring consistency.

3 Add ½ tsp salt, ½ tsp chilli powder and coriander. Keep aside.

4 Prepare the Sugam Paneer by heating 2 tbsp oil in a nonstick pan. Add ½ tsp salt, ½ tsp garam masala and ½ tsp red chilli powder. Remove from heat.

5 Add Sugam Paneer pieces a coriander. Mix gently with the oil.

6 Return to heat, fry for a few second Remove Sugam Paneer from pa Keep aside.

7 Heat a nonstick pan (not too ho smear 1 tsp oil in the centre.

8 Spread one karchhi (¼ cup) of batt to make a chillah of about 4" diamet

9 Pour some oil on the sides.

10 Turn over.

11 Heat one prepared Sugam Paneer piece on the side of the pan.

12 Remove chillah and Sugam Paneer from the pan.

13 Place the Sugam Paneer piece at one end of the chillah. Roll it up.

14 Serve hot with poodina chutney or any other sauce.

15 To make the next chillah, remove pan from heat. Cool the pan by sprinkling some water. Wipe clean.

16 Smear 1 tsp oil in the centre. Spread a karchhi of batter.

17 Return to heat and proceed as before. Serve hot.

Sugam Paneer Tikka Sandwiches

Toasted bread sandwiched with sauted slices of potatoes, Sugam Paneer and cabbage leaves.

Picture on facing page   *Makes 8 sandwiches*

INGREDIENTS

**8 cabbage leaves (take 1 small cabbage) -
each torn into 2 pieces
3-4 firm tomatoes - cut into slices
2 big boiled potatoes - sliced
250 gms/8 oz Sugam Paneer
salt and pepper to taste
cheese spread - enough to spread
3-4 tbsp butter
8 bread slices**

METHOD

1 Cut Sugam Paneer & potatoes into thin slices.

2 Heat 2 tbsp butter in a nonstick pan. Put a slice of potato on it and then shift to the side. Turn when the under side is light brown. Put more slices in the centre and brown them.

3 Repeat with all other potato slices. Let them be on the sides of the pan.

4 Put some more butter. Saute the Sugam Paneer slightly. Shift to the sides.

5 Place the cabbage leaves also on the hot pan. Remove from heat. Leave everything in the pan.

6   Lightly toast the bread slices. Spread cheese spread on one side and some butter on the other side of all slices.

7   On each toast spread some cabbage leaves on the cheese spread.

8   Cover the leaves with 2-3 potato slices. Sprinkle salt and pepper. Put Sugam Paneer slices over the potatoes. Put tomato slices over the Sugam Paneer.

9   Cover with another toasted slice, keeping the buttered side on the outside. Press gently. Keep aside till serving time.

10   To serve, heat on the pan till the bread turns crisp. Cut into 2 halves and serve with tomato ketchup or mustard sauce.

For more info, visit: www.sugampaneer.com

Cheesy Tomato Pasta

Picture on facing page   Serves 2

INGREDIENTS

**1½ cups unboiled pasta (penne or any
other pasta) - boiled (about 3 cups)
½ cup (50 gm/2 oz) - roughly mashed**
Sugam Paneer
**½ cup grated cheddar cheese - grated
¼ cup milk, approx.
1 small flower of broccoli (150 gms/5 oz)
3 tbsp olive oil or butter
2 onions - finely chopped
4-5 flakes of garlic- crushed
250 gm/8 oz tomatoes - blanched in hot
water, skinned and chopped finely
1 tomato - pureed in a mixer
8-10 basil leaves or tender tulsi leaves
1½ tsp salt, ½ tsp pepper
1 tsp dried oregano**

METHOD

1 Cut broccoli into very small florets with very
little stalk, (about 2 cups chopped).

2 For boiling pasta, boil 8 cups of water with 2
tsp salt. When the water starts to boil, add
pasta to the pan. Stir well. Boil for about 4-5
minutes till almost done. Remove from heat and
leave it in hot water for 2-3 minutes. Strain.

3 Add fresh water to refresh the pasta and strain
again. Sprinkle 1 tbsp olive oil on the pasta.
Keep aside.

4 To blanch tomatoes, put a cross on the
skin of the tomatoes. Put tomatoes in
a pan with some water. Boil for 2-3 minutes.
Remove from water and peel the skin of
tomatoes and chop finely.

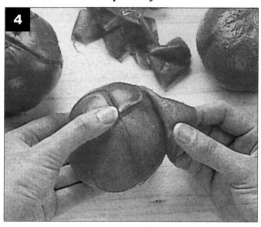

5 Heat 3 tbsp oil or butter. Add onion
and garlic, cook until onions turn soft.

6 Add tomatoes, fresh tomato puree,
basil leaves, salt, pepper and oregano.
Cook for 2 minutes, stirring occasionally.

7 Add broccoli, mix well for 1-2 minutes
till crisp-tender. Do not over cook. Keep
sauce aside. Let the broccoli be crisp and
crunchy.

8 At the time of serving, heat sauce, add
pasta, Sugam Paneer, cheese and milk.
Mix well. Remove from heat. Transfer to a
serving platter. Serve hot with garlic bread.

Chilli Sugam Paneer Dosa

Regular dosa with a different filling. Give it a try, you will forget the potato filling!

Picture on facing page Makes 10

INGREDIENTS

DOSA

½ cup parboiled rice (sela or ushna chaawal)
1¼ cups ordinary quality rice (permal chaawal)
½ cup dehusked black gram (dhuli urad dal)
1 tsp fenugreek seeds (methi dana)
1 tsp salt

TOMATO SPREAD

15 flakes garlic - crushed
¾ tsp red chilli paste or powder
1½ cups ready made tomato puree
6 tbsp tomato ketchup
1½ tsp oregano (dried)
salt and pepper to taste, 2 tbsp oil

CHILLI SUGAM PANEER

250 gms/8 oz Sugam Paneer - cut into ½" cubes
1½ capsicums - chopped
1½ tbsp soya sauce, 1½ tbsp vinegar
¾ tsp salt, ¾ tsp pepper
1½ tsp red chilli paste or red chilli powder
1½ tsp garlic paste (8 garlic flakes - crushed)

METHOD

1 Soak both rice, dal and fenugreek seeds together in a pan for atleast 6 hours.

2 Grind together finely to a paste, using some of the water in which it was soaked.

3 Add more water to the paste, if required, to get a paste of medium pouring consistency. Add salt. Mix well.

4 Keep aside for 12 hours or overnight in a warm place, to get fermented. After fermentation, the batter should rise a little and smell sour.

5 Mix Sugam Paneer with soya sauce, vinegar, salt, pepper, chilli paste and crushed garlic. Keep aside to marinate for 15 minutes.

6 Sprinkle some maida on the Sugam Paneer. Mix gently to coat. Deep fry till golden.

7 Crush the fried Sugam Paneer with fingers roughly. Add capsicum. Check salt.

8 To prepare the spread, heat 2 tbsp oil. Add garlic and cook till light brown. Add all the other ingredients and cook on low heat till it turns to a thick paste.

9 For dosas, mix the batter nicely with a karchhi, before preparing dosas.

10 Heat a non stick tawa on medium heat. Pour a tsp oil on the tawa. Sprinkle a pinch of salt on the oil. Rub the tawa with piece of onion or potato.

11 Remove tawa from heat & pour 1 heaped karchhi of batter. Spread quickly.

12 Return to heat. Cook the dosa a little.

13 Pour 2 tsp of oil upon the dosa and the sides. Cover for 1-2 minutes.

14 After it turns golden brown, gently loosen the sides and bottom.

15 Drop small dots of tomato spread, in different places on the dosa and spread quickly with the back of a spoon, covering the edges completely.

16 Put 3 tbsp of the filling in the centre of the dosa in a row and spread a little.

17 Fold over from both sides. Remove from tawa. Cut it from the middle diagonally to get 2 small pieces. Serve hot with coconut chutney.

Tip: For a party you can cut each dosa into four pieces diagonally like you do for a spring roll.

Mexican Fajita

Fa-hi-taa, (the letter 'j' is pronounced as 'h'). There is no hard and fast rule for making the roll of fajita. You can serve all the things together in a platter to the guests & ask them to make their own roll or wrap!

Makes 5-6

Picture on page 60

INGREDIENTS

7 FLOUR TORTILLAS
1½ cups plain flour (maida)
1 tsp baking powder, ½ tsp salt
warm water to knead

VEGETABLE FILLING
150 gms/5 oz Sugam Paneer - cut into ¼" thick,
long pieces
¼ of a small cauliflower - cut into small florets
½ of a small cabbage- shredded
½ cup French beans - sliced diagonally
2-3 carrots - sliced diagonally
1-2 dry, red chillies - crushed (¾ tsp red chilli
flakes)
1 tsp vinegar, ½ tsp salt
½ tsp freshly ground peppercorns
3 tbsp olive oil or any cooking oil, 1 tbsp butter
1 onion- sliced, 6 flakes garlic - crushed
2 tbsp chopped coriander
2 tsp white wine (optional)

SALAD
3-4 lettuce leaves - shredded
1- 2 green onions - chopped till the greens
½ tsp salt
1 tomato - chopped, 1 green chilli - chopped
½ cup cheddar cheese - grated (50 gms/2 oz)

SOUR CREAM
¾ cup thick yogurt - hang for ½ hour in a cloth
½ cup whipping cream
few drops Tabasco sauce, salt to taste

SALSA
5 tomatoes - roasted, 1 tbsp oil
2 onions - chopped finely
2 green chillies - chopped
2 tbsp chopped coriander
1 tbsp tomato ketchup, 1 tsp vinegar
½ tsp salt and ¼ tsp pepper, or to taste

METHOD

1 Sift maida with baking powder and salt. Add warm water very gradually and bind together roughly. Knead with wet hands till a smooth & elastic dough is ready.

2 Make 7 equal balls. Cover with a plastic wrap or a cling film or a damp cloth and keep aside for 15 minutes.

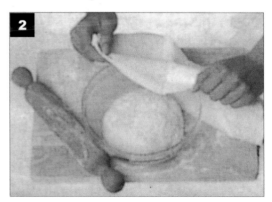

3 Roll out each ball into a tortilla, using a little maida till you get a very thin round of about 8-9" diameter.

8 For salsa, pierce a tomato with a fork. Broil in an oven till the skin turns blackish and charred. Roast all the tomatoes like this. Cool the tomatoes and peel. Chop 2 tomatoes and puree the other 3 tomatoes. Heat oil and saute onions and green chillies till onion turns soft. Add all other ingredients of the salsa & cook for 2-3 minutes. Remove from heat.

4 Heat a tawa (griddle). Cook lightly on one side for about a minute and then turn. Reduce heat and cook the other side also for a minute till light brown specks appear. Wrap in an aluminium foil and keep aside in a casserole. Make all tortillas similarly.

9 To prepare the filling, heat 2 tbsp oil and 1 tbsp butter. Cook onions and garlic till soft. Except Sugam Paneer add all the marinated vegetables. Stir- fry for 5-7 minutes on moderate heat till tender but still remain crisp. Add coriander, wine, Sugam Paneer, ¾ tsp salt and ½ tsp pepper or to taste. Cook for 2-3 minutes. Remove from heat.

5 For the filling, mix Sugam Paneer, cauliflower, cabbage, beans, carrots, red chilli flakes, salt, pepper, 1 tbsp oil and vinegar. Keep aside for half an hour in the refrigerator.

10 To serve, put sour cream, salad and salsa in separate bowls. Serve tortillas wrapped in a napkin in a casserole or basket.

6 For salad, mix all ingredients of the salad in a bowl. Mix well.

11 Serve the vegetable filling separately in a sizzler plate.

12 Make your own roll. Take one tortilla, spread 1-2 tsp of the sour cream on the whole tortilla spreading till the sides, then spread some vegetables on it, then sprinkle some salad and finally pour 1½ tbsp salsa. Roll and enjoy.

7 For sour cream, beat hung curd, salt, tabasco sauce and cream till smooth and thick. Keep aside.

Naaza

A great combination of Pizza & Naan! Naan spread with an Indian tomato spread flavoured with kasoori methi, topped with Sugam Paneer tikkas and mozzarella cheese & grilled in the oven.

Picture on facing page   *Serves 4*

INGREDIENTS

2 ready made naans
100-150 gms/4-5 oz mozzarella cheese

TOMATO SPREAD
1-2 tbsp oil, 4 flakes garlic - crushed
2 small tomatoes - pureed in a mixer
¼ tsp salt, ¼ tsp garam masala
¼ tsp red chilli powder
2 tbsp tomato sauce
2 tsp dry fenugreek leaves (kasoori methi)

SUGAM PANEER TOPPING
100 gms/4 oz Sugam Paneer - cut into ¼" pieces
2 tsp dry fenugreek leaves (kasoori methi)
½ green and ½ yellow capsicum - cut into ½" squares, or 1 green one
1 tomato - cut into 4 pieces, deseeded and cut into ½" pieces
½ onion - cut into ½" squares
¼ tsp each - salt, red chilli powder, haldi and garam masala, or to taste
1 tbsp tomato puree
½ tsp ginger-garlic paste

YOGURT CHUTNEY (Mix Everything Together)
2 tbsp mint paste (hari chutney)
3 tbsp yogurt
a pinch of kala namak and bhuna jeera
1 tsp oil or cream

METHOD

1 For the tomato spread, heat oil. Add garlic and all other ingredients. Cook till thick.

2 For the Sugam Paneer topping, he 1½ tbsp oil. Add onion. Saute golden. Reduce heat. Add salt, red ch powder, haldi and garam masala. Mix. A tomato puree and ginger- garlic paste. A capsicums and tomato. Mix.

3 Add Sugam Paneer and kasoori met Mix well and remove from heat.

4 Brush naan with 1 tsp oil. Spread son tomato spread, covering well till t edges.

5 Sprinkle some mozzarella chees Spread Sugam Paneer toppin Sprinkle some cheese again.

6 Grill for about 15 minutes at 180°C/350°F till the Sugam Paneer gets grilled and the edges of the naan turn brown. Do not over grill, it turns hard!

7 Cut into rectangular pieces and serve hot with yogurt chutney.

For more info, visit: **www.sugampaneer.com**

Deep Dish Quiche

Picture on facing page   Serves 6

INGREDIENTS

SHELL
¼ cup melted butter
1¼ cups plain flour (maida)
a pinch of baking powder
¼ cup grated cheddar cheese
3 tbsp water, or as required

VEGETABLES FOR FILLING
1 cup corn kernels (freshly boiled or tinned)
2 cups sliced mushrooms
1 cup grated Sugam Paneer
1 onion - finely chopped
½ tsp salt and ¼ tsp pepper
1 tbsp butter - softened

MIX TOGETHER
4 tbsp cream, ¼ cup tomato puree
1½ tbsp cornflour
½ tsp salt, ¼ tsp freshly ground pepper
2 tbsp chopped fresh parsley or coriander

OTHER INGREDIENTS
1½ cups (150 gm/5 oz) grated mozzarella or
pizza cheese
½ tsp dried oregano, a few tomato slices

2 Roll out to a thin chappati, slightly bigger than the baking flan tin (a shallow tin with a loose bottom), such that the chapati covers a little on the sides. Roll out and place it in the baking flan tin. Press the mixture well to cover the base and the sides too. Press carefully to get a well levelled base. Trim the excess by rolling a rolling pin on the edges of the tin.

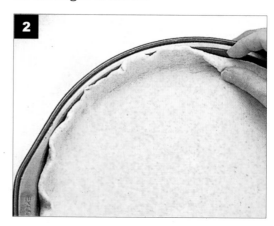

METHOD

1 Sift flour and baking powder. Combine butter with flour, rubbing well until it looks like bread crumbs. Add cheese. Add just enough water to bind and knead lightly to a firm dough. Chill the dough, well covered in a wet muslin cloth for 30 minutes.

3 Prick with a fork all over to avoid the crust from puffing up during baking.

4 Bake the quiche crusts in a hot oven (200°C/ 390°F), for about 10-15 minutes, until light golden yellow. Allow to cool.

5 To prepare the filling, heat butter. Add onions. Cook till soft. Add mushrooms and cook until water evaporates and they turn dry. Add corn kernels and Sugam Paneer. Add ½ tsp salt and ¼ tsp pepper. Cook for a few seconds. Remove from heat.

6 In a cup, mix together – cream, tomato puree, cornflour, salt, pepper and parsley.

7 Spoon the mushroom-Sugam Paneer mix into a cooled quiche crust and level it.

8 Sprinkle ¼ cup grated cheese on it, keeping some for the top.

9 Spread the cream-tomato puree mixture on the cheese. Sprinkle with the remaining cheese.

10 Sprinkle some oregano. Arrange a few halved slices of tomato.

11 Bake in a preheated oven set at 190°C/375°F for about 25 minutes or until the filling is set and the top is golden. Allow to cool before serving.

For more info, visit: www.sugampaneer.com

INDIAN
MEAL TIME DISHES
DRY & MASALA

Tandoori Platter with BBQ Sauce

The platter looks equally appetizing without the wooden skewers!

Picture on facing page   Serves 8

INGREDIENTS

250 gm/8 oz Sugam Paneer - cut into large (1½") cubes
2 capsicums - cut into large cubes
8 cherry tomatoes or 1 large tomato - cut into 8 pieces & pulp removed
200 gm/6 oz (10-12) mushrooms - trim ends of the stalks, leaving them whole
100 gm/4 oz baby corns - blanched with a pinch of haldi and 1 tsp salt in 3 cups water
1 onion - cut into quarters & separated

MARINADE
1 cup thick yogurt - hang for 30 minutes
2 tbsp thick cream, 2 tbsp oil
1 tbsp cornflour
1 tbsp thick ginger-garlic paste
½ tsp black salt
¼ tsp haldi or tandoori food colour
2 tsp tandoori masala (barbecue masala)
½ tsp red chilli powder
¾ tsp salt or to taste

BARBECUE SAUCE
3 tbsp butter, 4-5 flakes garlic - crushed
2 large tomatoes - pureed till smooth
¼ cup ready made tomato puree
¼ tsp red chilli powder, ½ tsp pepper
¾ tsp salt or to taste, ¼ tsp sugar
½ tsp worcestershire sauce, ½ tsp soya sauce

METHOD

1. Rub oil generously on a wire rack or grill of the oven.

2. Mix all ingredients of the marinade. Add Sugam Paneer, mushrooms and baby corns to the marinade and mix well to coat the marinade. Remove from bowl and arrange on the rack or on greased wooden skewers. In the remaining marinade which is sticking to the sides of the bowl, add onion, capsicum and tomatoes. Leave these in the bowl itself. Marinate all for atleast ½ hour.

3. Grill Sugam Paneer and vegetables in the oven at 210°C/410°F for 12-15 minutes or roast in a gas tandoor, on the wire rack or on skewers. Spoon a little oil/ melted butter (basting) on them. Add onion, capsicum and tomatoes. Grill for another 5-7 minutes.

4. For the barbecue sauce, heat oil in a kadhai. Add garlic. Stir for 30 seconds. Add tomatoes, tomato puree and red chilli powder. Cook for 5 minutes till well blended. Add all other ingredients and ½ cup water to get a thin sauce. Boil. Simmer for 2 minutes. Remove from heat and keep aside.

5. To serve, put some hot sauce on the serving plate. Arrange grilled vegetables on the sauce with or without skewers. Pour some hot sauce over the vegetables. Serve at once. You may serve the platter on rice too.

68

Tawa Sugam Paneer

A unique preparation of Sugam Paneer cooked on a tawa.

Picture on facing page   *Serves 4*

MARINATE FOR 15 MINUTES
400 gms/13 oz Sugam Paneer - cut into big (1")
cubes
½ tsp red chilli powder
½ tsp haldi
½ tsp salt, 1 tsp chaat masala

MASALA
½ tsp carom seeds (ajwain seeds)
½ tsp cumin seeds (jeera)
1 large onion - chopped
3 tsp garlic paste
2 green chillies - chopped
2 tsp coriander (dhania) powder
½ tsp red chilli powder
½ tsp salt, or to taste
2 tomatoes - chopped
1 capsicum - chopped
¼ tsp garam masala
¼ tsp black cumin (shah jeera)

METHOD

1 Cut Sugam Paneer into big, thick pieces. Sprinkle red chilli powder, haldi, salt and chaat masala. Mix well to coat all sides of paneer with the powdered masalas. Keep the marinated paneer aside for 15 minutes.

2 Heat 2 tbsp oil on a non stick tawa a pan. Shallow fry the Sugam Pane on the tawa, turning sides, till light brown on all sides.

3 For the masala, heat 3 tbsp oil in kadhai. When oil is hot, add ajwa and jeera. Let jeera turn golden.

4 Add the chopped onion and stir t golden.

5 Reduce heat. Add garlic paste, gree chillies, coriander powder, red chi powder, and salt. Fry on medium heat for few seconds.

6 Add chopped tomatoes. Stir fry for 5-7 minutes till the oil separates. Keep aside.

7 Mix in the fried Sugam Paneer, capsicum, garam masala and shah jeera. Mix and cook for 1-2 minutes. Serve hot.

Hari Chutney Sugam Paneer

Chatpata Sugam Paneer dish which goes very well as a side dish.

Picture on facing page   *Serves 4*

INGREDIENTS

200 gms/6 oz Sugam Paneer - cut into about
1" big triangular pieces of ¼" thickness
1½ cups of yogurt - hang in a muslin cloth for
20 minutes
4 flakes garlic and ½" piece of ginger - crush
to a paste or, 1 tsp ginger-garlic paste
¼ tsp cumin seeds (jeera), 3 tbsp oil
1 onion - sliced thinly
¾ tsp chaat masala - to sprinkle on
Sugam Paneer

CHUTNEY (GRIND TOGETHER)
½ cup poodina (mint)
½ cup green coriander (hara dhania)
2 green chillies, 1 onion
½ tsp black salt (kala namak)
½ tsp roasted cumin (bhuna jeera)
½ tsp salt or to taste
¼ tsp powdered sugar

METHOD

1 Hang yogurt in a muslin cloth for 20 minutes.

2 For chutney, wash coriander and mint leaves.

3 Grind together all the ingredients given under chutney to a paste. Keep the chutney aside.

4 Beat hung yogurt well till smooth.

5 To the hung yogurt, add the chutney. Keep aside.

6 Cut the block of Sugam Paneer into rectangular slices of about ¼" thickness. Now cut each slice into 2 triangular pieces. Do not make the pieces too thick.

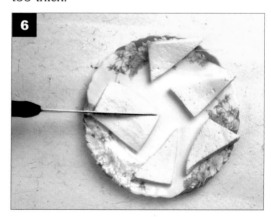

7 Cut each piece further into 2 triangles if the piece is big. Sprinkle chaat masala on the Sugam Paneer. Mix gently.

8 Heat oil in a kadhai, add jeera and ginger-garlic paste. Cook for few seconds.

9 Add sliced onion and cook till golden.

10 Reduce heat and add the yogurt-chutney. Cook for 2-3 minutes on low heat, stirring in between. Check salt. Keep aside.

11 At the time of serving, add Sugam Paneer pieces to the chutney and mix gently but thoroughly to coat the pieces nicely with chutney. Heat on low heat. Serve.

Sugam Paneer Jalfrezi

Sugam Paneer deliciously combined with mixed vegetables.

Picture on facing page Serves 4

Picture on facing page

INGREDIENTS

150 gm/5 oz Sugam Paneer - cut into thin long pieces, 1 large carrot - peeled
8-10 french beans - sliced diagonally into 1" pieces
½ green capsicum - deseed and cut into thin fingers
½ yellow or red pepper (capsicum) - deseeded and sliced into thin fingers
½ cup boiled peas
1 long, firm tomato - cut into 4, pulp removed and cut into thin long pieces
15-20 curry leaves, 3 tbsp oil

COLLECT TOGETHER
½ tsp cumin seeds (jeera)
¼ tsp mustard seeds (sarson)
¼ tsp onion seeds (kalonji)
¼ tsp fenugreek seeds (methi daana)

MIX TOGETHER
½ cup tomato puree
1 tsp tomato ketchup
2 tsp ginger-garlic paste or
2 tsp ginger-garlic - finely chopped
½ tsp red chilli powder
1 tsp coriander powder (dhania powder)
½ tsp amchoor powder (dry mango powder)
1 tsp salt

METHOD

1 Mix together - tomato puree, tomato ketchup, ginger-garlic, red chilli powder, dhania powder, amchoor and salt in a cup. Keep aside.

2 Cut carrot diagonally into thin slices.

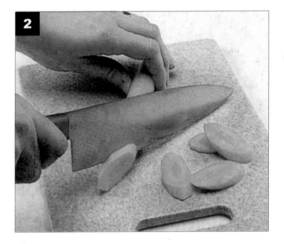

3 Heat 3 tbsp oil in a kadhai. Add the collected seeds together. When jeera turns golden, reduce heat and add curry leaves and stir for a few seconds.

4 Add the tomato puree mixed with dry masalas and stir on medium heat for 2 minutes.

5 Add carrot and beans. Stir for 1 minute.

74

6 Add ¼ cup water. Cover the kadhai. Cook on low heat for about 4-5 minutes, till vegetables are cooked but still remain crunchy.

7 Add the capsicums, boiled peas, Sugam Paneer and tomato slices. Stir till well blended. Remove from heat. Serve hot.

Sugam Paneer Spring Onion

Sugam Paneer with green onions/scallions.

Picture on facing page   *Serves 4*

INGREDIENTS

200 gms/6 oz Sugam Paneer - cut into 1" pieces
200 gms/6 oz spring onions - cut white bulb into
rings and cut greens diagonally into
½" pieces, keep greens separate
1 green chilli - deseeded & chopped
4 tbsp oil
6-8 flakes garlic - crushed, ¼ tsp haldi
2 tomatoes - pureed in a mixer
2 tomatoes - finely chopped
1 tbsp tomato ketchup
3 cloves (laung) - crushed roughly
2 tsp coriander (dhania) powder
1¼ tsp salt, or to taste
½ tsp red chilli powder
½ tsp garam masala
4 tbsp fresh cream or ¼ cup milk

METHOD

1 Cut white bulb of spring onion into rings and cut green part diagonally into ½" pieces.

2 Heat 4 tbsp oil in a kadhai. Add garlic. Saute for 1 minute on low heat. Add the white of onions and stir fry till light brown.

3 Add ¼ tsp haldi. Stir for 1 minute.

4 Add fresh tomato puree and chopped tomatoes and stir fry for 5-7 minutes, till they turn almost dry.

7 Reduce heat. Add dhania powder, salt, red chilli powder and garam masala. Cook for 2 minutes on low heat.

8 Add ¼ cup water. Boil. Add the Sugam Paneer, greens of onions and chopped green chilli. Cook for 1-2 minutes on low heat till well mixed.

9 Keeping the heat low, add cream or milk. Mix. Remove from heat and serve hot.

Note: If spring onions are not available, use 1 capsicum cut into thin long pieces and 2 small, ordinary onions cut into thin rings.

5 Add tomato ketchup. Stir to mix well.

6 Add crushed laung. Cook for ½ minute.

77

Sugam Paneer Kadhai Waala

A semi-dry Sugam Paneer preparation flavoured with coriander and fenugreek.

Picture on facing page   Serves 4-5

Picture on facing page

INGREDIENTS

125 gms/4 oz Sugam Paneer - cut into fingers
3 large capsicums - cut into fingers
3 tbsp oil
½ tsp cumin seeds (jeera)
2 onions - cut into rings and then into halves
1 tsp ginger or garlic paste
4 tomatoes - ground to a puree in a mixer
¼ tsp turmeric (haldi)
1¼ tsp salt
¼ tsp dry mango powder (amchoor)
1 tsp coriander powder (dhania)
½ tsp garam masala
¼ tsp red chilli powder
2 tbsp dry fenugreek leaves (kasoori methi)
¾ cup water
½ cup milk

METHOD

1 Cut Sugam Paneer and capsicum into thin fingers.

2 Heat oil in a kadhai. Add jeera. Let it turn golden.

3 Add onions and cook till soft.

4 Add ginger or garlic paste and stir for 30 seconds.

5 Add pureed tomatoes and stir till puree turns dry.

6 Add haldi, salt, amchoor, dhania powder, garam masala, red chilli powder and kasoori methi. Stir till oil separates.

7 Add ¾ cup water mix well.

8 Add capsicum and stir for 1 minute.

9 Add Sugam Paneer. Mix well gently.

10 Reduce heat and add milk, stirring continuously. Remove from heat and serve hot.

For more info, visit: www.sugampaneer.com

Tikka Sugam Paneer Subzi

A grilled Sugam Paneer dish which is relished with meals as a side dish.

Picture on facing page   *Serves 4*

INGREDIENTS

250 gms/8 oz Sugam Paneer - cut into 1" cubes
¾ tsp salt, ¼ tsp red chilli powder
¼ tsp turmeric powder (haldi) or a pinch of red food colour
1 tsp lemon juice, 1 tbsp oil
2 capsicums - cut into fine rings
2 onions - cut into fine rings
¼ tsp black salt (kala namak)
¼ tsp salt
2 tsp tandoori masala

GRIND TO A ROUGH PASTE WITHOUT ANY WATER
3-4 flakes garlic - optional
1½" piece ginger, 2-3 green chillies
1 tsp cumin seeds (jeera)

METHOD

1 Cut capsicum and onion into fine rings.

2 Grind garlic, ginger, green chillies, jeera to a thick rough paste. Do not add water.

3 Add ¾ tsp salt, chilli powder and lemon juice to the paste. Add a little haldi or food colour to give colour to the paste.

4 Cut Sugam Paneer into 1" squares. Apply ¾ of the ginger-chilli paste nicely on all the pieces. Keep the left over paste aside.

5 Place this Sugam Paneer on a greased wire rack of an oven and grill for 10-15 minutes till it is dry and slightly crisp. Keep aside till serving time.

6 At serving time, heat 1 tbsp oil in a kadhai. Fry onion and capsicum rings for a few minutes till onions turn transparent.

7 Add the left over ginger-chilli paste and a few drops of lemon juice. Add black salt and ¼ tsp salt too.

8 Add grilled Sugam Paneer pieces. Sprinkle tandoori masala. Toss for a minute till the Sugam Paneer turns soft and is heated properly. Serve immediately.

Sugam Paneer Amravati

Onion and coconut shreds coat Sugam Paneer fingers in a South Indian style.

Picture on facing page   Serves 4-6

INGREDIENTS

200 gm/6 oz Sugam Paneer - cut into thin fingers
5 onions - 2 grated and 3 sliced
½ cup curry leaves
1½ tsp brown small mustard seeds (rai)
½ cup fresh coconut - grated finely
a pinch of tandoori red food colour
1¼ tsp salt, or to taste
3 tbsp lemon juice (juice of 1 lemon)

RED CHILLI PASTE
4 Kashmiri dry, red chillies - deseeded and
soaked in warm water for 10 minutes
1" piece ginger
1 tbsp cashews (kaju)
3 tbsp yogurt
2 tsp coriander powder (dhania powder)
2-3 cloves (laung)
6-7 peppercorns (saboot kali mirch)

3   Scrape brown skin of ¼ of a coconut
     and grate finely to get ½ cup grated
coconut.

METHOD

1   Grate 2 onions.

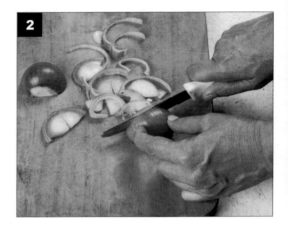

2   Cut the other 3 onions into halves. Then cut
     each half widthwise into half-rings to get thin
strips of onion.

4   Drain the soaked red chillies. Add all
     other ingredients of the paste and grind
to a smooth paste using a little water for
grinding.

5	Heat 6 tbsp oil. Add rai. Let it splutter for a minute.	10	Add food colour and salt.
6	Add grated onions and curry leaves. Cook till onions turn light brown.	11	Add 1 cup water. Boil.
7	Add onion slices and cook for 3-4 minutes till soft.	12	Add Sugam Paneer and mix well.
8	Add coconut & cook on low heat for 5 minutes till crisp. Keep it spread out while cooking.	13	Cook on low heat for 5 minutes, stirring occasionally.
9	Add red chilli paste & stir fry for 2-3 minutes.	14	Add lemon juice and mix well. Serve hot.

INDIAN
MEAL TIME DISHES
GRAVIES & CURRIES

Broccoli Bonanza

Serves 4　　　　　　　　　　　　*Picture on page 86*

INGREDIENTS

**250 gm/8 oz Sugam Paneer (take a square
shaped whole block of Sugam Paneer
weighing 250 gms/8 oz)
salt, red chilli powder and chat masala
to sprinkle**

**CURRY
2 tbsp oil
1 onion - sliced
2 tbsp curry powder
2 tbsp finely chopped coriander
2 cups milk
1 tsp salt, or to taste
2 tsp cornflour mixed with 1 tbsp water**

**FILLING
½ cup grated broccoli
½ tsp ginger- garlic paste
½ of a small onion- chopped
½ tsp salt, ½ tsp pepper
½ tsp tomato sauce**

METHOD

1　Cut Sugam Paneer into 4 big pieces and then divide each piece to get 8 equal square pieces. With the help of a knife from the centre of each piece scoop out the Sugam Paneer forming a square shaped hollow. Leave a border of ¼" all around. Do not dig very deep. Let the bottom be intact. Keep the scooped out Sugam Paneer aside.

2　Sprinkle salt, chilli powder and chat masala on all sides of Sugam Paneer. Keep aside.

3　For the curry, heat 2 tbsp oil in a small, heavy pan. Reduce heat. Add onion and stir till golden. Add curry powder and fresh coriander and stir for a few seconds.

4　Add 2 tbsp of the crushed scooped Sugam Paneer and 1 tsp salt. Mix well.

5　Remove pan from heat and add milk, stirring continuously. Return the pan to heat and stir until the sauce comes to a boil. Boil for 1 minute, stirring continuously.

6 Add cornflour mixed with water and stir for 2 minutes on low heat till slightly thick. Remove from heat. Keep curry aside.

7 For filling, heat 1 tbsp oil in a pan, add ginger-garlic paste. Wait for a minute.

8 Add onion and cook till golden. Add broccoli. Mix.

9 Add salt, pepper and tomato ketchup. Cook for a minute. Remove from heat.

10 Heat 2 tbsp oil in a pan. Fry gently 4 pieces of Sugam Paneer blocks at a time. Fry turning all the sides till golden.

11 Remove on paper napkins. Fill 1 tsp of filling in each scooped out block.

12 In a shallow rectangular serving dish, put the hot gravy. Arrange the stuffed Sugam Paneer blocks on the gravy. Cover and heat in an oven or a microwave. Serve.

Note: If using a microwave, cover loosely with a cling film and micro high for 2 minutes. If using an ordinary oven, cover loosely with aluminium foil and heat for 5-8 minutes in a moderately hot oven at 180°C/350°F till hot.

Rajasthani Bharwaan Lauki

Roundels of bottle gourd stuffed with Sugam Paneer.

Serves 6   *Picture on opposite page*

INGREDIENTS

500 gm/16 oz (1lb) bottle gourd (lauki) - choose lauki of medium thickness

FILLING
200 gm/6 oz Sugam Paneer - crumbled (mash roughly)
1 tsp finely chopped ginger
1 green chilli - finely chopped
2 tbsp chopped green coriander
8-10 cashewnuts (kaju) - chopped
8-10 raisins (kishmish) - soaked in water
¾ tsp salt or to taste

MASALA
2 tbsp oil or ghee
2 cloves (laung), 2 bay leaves (tej patta)
seeds of 2 green cardamoms (chhoti illaichi)
1" stick cinnamon (dalchini)

TOMATO PASTE (GRIND TOGETHER)
3 tomatoes
1 green chilli
½" piece ginger
½ tsp red chilli powder
1 tsp dhania powder
¼ tsp haldi, ¾ tsp salt
½ tsp jeera (cumin seeds), ¼ tsp sugar

METHOD

1 Peel lauki. Cut vertically into two pieces from the centre to get 2 smaller pieces.

2 Boil in salted water, covered, for about 10 minutes, till done. Remove from water and cool.

3 Scoop seeds from both the pieces of the lauki and make them hollow.

4 For filling - Mix Sugam Paneer, ginger, green chilli, coriander, kaju, kishmish and salt.

5 Stuff it into the boiled lauki pieces. Keep aside.

6 For masala- heat ghee/oil. Add laung, seeds of chhoti illaichi, dalchini and tej patta. Stir for a minute.

7 Add the prepared tomato paste. Stir for 3-4 minutes till thick and oil separates.

8 Add 1½ cups water. Boil. Simmer for 4-5 minutes till oil separates. Keep aside.

9 At serving time, saute whole lauki pieces in a non stick pan in 1 tbsp oil, turning sides carefully to brown from all sides. Remove from pan.

10 Pour half of the hot gravy in a dish. Cut the lauki into ¾" thick round pieces and arrange over the gravy. Pour the remaining hot tomato gravy on top. Serve.

Matar Sugam Paneer Curry

The most common dish of Punjab, but yet liked by everyone.

Serves 4   *Picture on page 92*

INGREDIENTS

200 gms/7 oz Sugam Paneer - cut into 1" cubes
1 cup shelled peas (matar)

GROUND TOGETHER
¼ cup well beaten yogurt (beat till smooth
with a wire whisk)
2 onions, 1" piece ginger
3 tomatoes
2 cloves (laung)
seeds of 1 brown cardamoms (moti illaichi)
1 tsp coriander (dhania) powder
½ tsp red chilli powder, ¼ tsp amchoor
¼ tsp garam masala
4-5 tbsp oil

METHOD

1 Grind onions, ginger, tomato, laung and moti illaichi to a smooth puree in a mixer.

2 Heat oil in a kadhai. Add the onion - tomato puree. Cook covered on high heat for about 5 minutes till quite dry. Remove cover and cook, stirring frequently for 5-7 minutes till very thick and absolutely dry.

3 Add dhania powder, red chilli powder, amchoor and garam masala. Reduce heat and cook for 5 minutes more till oil separates. The masala should be dry and look glossy because the oil separates which makes the masala as well as the sides of the kadhai turn glossy.

4 Beat yogurt with a wire whisk or fork till very smooth.

5 Add well beaten yogurt to the masala, stir continuously for about 3-4 minutes, till oil separates again and the masala turns to a bright red colour.

6 Add enough water, about 2½ cups water, to get a thick gravy. Add salt to taste, about 1 tsp salt. Cover and cook the gravy for about 5 minutes on low heat till oil separates and comes to the surface.

7 Add peas. Cook covered till peas are done.

8 Add Sugam Paneer and ¼ tsp garam masala. Cook on low heat for 3-4 minutes till Sugam Paneer gets soft. Serve hot.

Has the oil separated from the masala? Is it time to add water or should I stir fry the masala some more?

Sometimes when we do not add too much oil for home cooked meals, the oil actually does not separate and float on the surface. So, when the masala stops sticking to the bottom of the kadhai and starts to collect in the centre as a ball, it is done. The sides of the kadhai or the pan get glossy with oil too. Go ahead and add water to get the gravy.

Mewa Seekh in Gravy

Do not get put off by the long list of ingredients, the final product is delicious. The seekhs are simple to make and the ingredients are easily available! The gravy can also be used with simply fried Sugam Paneer, or baby corns or any koftas.

Serves 4 Picture on page 94

INGREDIENTS

¾ cups grated Sugam Paneer (75 gms/3 oz)
a few toothpicks
¼ cup dry bread crumbs
1 tsp cornflour
¼ tsp garam masala, ¼- ½ tsp salt or to taste
¼ tsp red chilli powder, a pinch of amchoor

DRY ROAST ON A TAWA
1 tsp sunflower seeds (chironji) or
1 tsp chopped almonds (badam)
1 tsp melon seeds (magaz)

PASTE (GRIND TOGETHER)
½" piece ginger, 3-4 flakes garlic
1 green chilli
3 tbsp green coriander
5 cashewnuts (kaju), 4 almonds (badam)
3 raisins (kishmish)
2-3 whole pistachio (pistas)
¼ tsp nutmeg (jaiphal)
¼ tsp mace (javetri)

GRAVY
2 onions & ½" piece of ginger and 3-4 flakes
of garlic - ground to a paste together
4 tbsp dry fenugreek leaves (kasoori methi)
½ cup fresh cream or thin malai
3 tbsp oil
1 tbsp butter
1 tsp salt, or to taste
½ tsp red chilli powder
½ tsp garam masala, a pinch of amchoor
1 cup milk (approx.)

CRUSH TOGETHER
½" stick cinnamon (dalchini)
seeds of 2-3 green cardamom (chhoti illaichi)
3-4 cloves (laung)
4-5 peppercorns (saboot kali mirch)
2 tbsp cashewnuts (kaju)

METHOD

1 Roast magaz and chironji/almonds on a tawa on low heat. Cool.

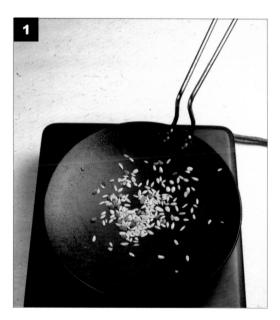

2 Grind all the ingredients given under paste in a mixer to a paste.

3 Mix together - ¼ cup bread crumbs, cornflour, garam masala, salt, red chilli powder, amchoor, grated Sugam Paneer, roasted chironji/almonds, magaz, and the prepared paste. Mix well.

4 Take a lemon sized ball of the mixture. Make a small roll of 1½" length. Flatten it from the sides. Insert a toothpick from one flattened end to the other, going straight out of the roll. Repeat with the left over mixture. Keep the seekhs covered with a cling wrap in the refrigerator for at least ½ hour so that they get set properly.

5 Grind all the ingredients given under 'Crush Together' on a chakla belan or in a small spice grinder. Keep aside the crushed powder.

6 For the gravy, grind onions, ginger and garlic together to a paste. Heat 3 tbsp oil and 1 tbsp butter. Add onion-garlic paste and cook on low heat till oil separates. Do not let the onions turn brown.

7 Add the freshly ground masala-kaju powder. Cook for a few seconds.

8 Add kasoori methi and cream, cook on low heat for 2-3 minutes till cream dries up.

9 Add salt, red chilli powder, garam masala and amchoor. Stir for 1 minute.

10 Add 1 cup milk and ½ cup water. Boil for 1 minute on low heat. Remove from heat.

11 Heat oil in a kadhai. Remove seekhs from the fridge. Deep fry 2-3 seekhs at a time alongwith the toothpicks till golden brown. Drain on paper napkins. Keep aside till serving time.

12 At serving time, heat sticks and gravy separately. Pour the hot gravy in a serving dish and arrange the hot sticks over it. If you want, put some gravy in the serving dish, arrange seekhs and again pour the rest of the gravy on top. If you like, you can heat the seekhs in gravy together, in a microwave. Serve hot.

Matar Malai Sugam Paneer

Picture on facing page   *Serves 4*

INGREDIENTS

125 gms/4 oz Sugam Paneer - cut into ¼" pieces
1½ cups shelled, boiled peas
1 tbsp cashewnuts (kaju) - grind to a
fine powder
1 onion - ground to a paste
¼ tsp pepper powder,
preferably white pepper
½ cup (75 gms/3 oz) cream (malai) - whip with
½ cup milk till smooth
4 tbsp dry fenugreek leaves (kasoori methi)
salt to taste, a pinch of sugar
½ cup milk (approx.)

CRUSH TOGETHER
½ stick cinnamon (dalchini)
3-4 cloves (laung)
2 cardamoms (moti illaichi)

METHOD

1 Crush together dalchini, laung and seeds of moti illaichi on a chakla-belan (rolling board and pin). Keep the masala aside.

2 Heat 2 tbsp oil. Add onion paste and cook on low heat till oil separates. Do not let the onion turn brown.

3 Add the crushed spices and pepper powder. Cook for a few seconds.

4 Add kasoori methi and malai, cook on low heat for 2-3 minutes till malai dries up slightly.

5 Add boiled peas and Sugam Paneer.

6 Add powdered kajus and cook for a few seconds.

7 Add enough milk to get a thick gravy. Add salt and sugar to taste. Bring to a boil.

8 Serve garnished with some kajus roasted on a tawa till golden.

Basil Tomato Sugam Paneer

Sugam Paneer in a tomato gravy flavoured with basil.

Picture on facing page   Serves 6

INGREDIENTS

300 gms/10 oz Sugam Paneer
4 large tomatoes - blanched, peeled & pureed
1 tbsp oil
1 large onion - chopped finely
8 laung (cloves) - crushed
10-12 peppercorns (saboot kali mirch) - crushed coarsely

MARINADE
1½ cups yogurt
2 tsp cornflour
a few basil leaves - finely chopped (2 tbsp)
1½-2 tsp salt
¾ tsp red chilli powder

OTHER INGREDIENTS
2-3 tsp tomato ketchup
1 tsp butter
1 tsp tandoori masala

3 Pit a cross on the tomatoes. Boil in water for 2-3 minutes. Remove from water. Remove its peel and grind to a puree in the blender.

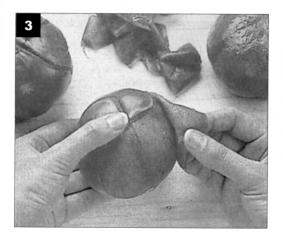

METHOD

1 Cut Sugam Paneer into 1 inch pieces.

2 Mix all ingredients of the marinade and marinate the Sugam Paneer in it.

4 Heat oil in a pan. Add the onions and laung. Stir fry for a few minutes till the onions turn light brown.

5 Add the prepared tomato puree, tomato ketchup, butter and tandoori masala. Cook for 5-7 minutes till absolutely dry. Remove from heat and let it cool. Keep aside till serving time.

6 At serving time, add the marinated Sugam Paneer with all the yogurt to the tomato-onion masala. Cook on low heat for a few minutes till you get the desired gravy. Do not over cook. (The curd might curdle if the heat is too high or if the gravy is kept for too long on heat.)

7 Transfer to a serving dish. Sprinkle with crushed peppercorns. Garnish with chopped basil leaves.

For more info, visit: www.sugampaneer.com

Piste Waala Sugam Paneer

A rich Mughlai style of cooking Sugam Paneer with pista paste, giving the curry a lovely green colour and flavour.

Picture on facing page   *Serves 6*

Picture on facing page

INGREDIENTS

300 gm/10 oz Sugam Paneer - cut into 1" pieces
2 large onions
½ cup curd - beat well till smooth
2 tsp ginger-garlic paste or 1" ginger piece &
4-5 flakes garlic - crushed to a paste
1 tbsp dhania powder, 1 tsp salt, or to taste
½ tsp pepper powder, preferably white
pepper powder, ½ cup fresh cream
½ tsp garam masala powder

GRIND TOGETHER TO A PASTE WITH
¼ CUP WATER
½ cup pistachio nuts (pistas) with the hard cover-skinned, soaked and peeled
1 green chilli - finely chopped
¼ cup chopped fresh coriander

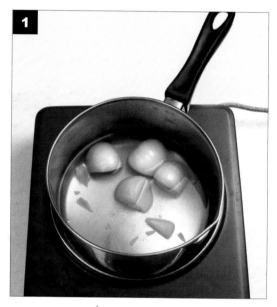

METHOD

1 Peel and cut onions into 4 pieces. Boil in 1 cup water for 2-3 minutes. Drain, cool slightly and grind to a fine paste. Keep boiled onion paste aside.

2 Soak pista in hot water for 10 minutes, drain and peel. Reserve a few peeled pistachio nuts for garnish.

100

3 Grind remaining peeled pistas with chopped green chillies and coriander to a fine green paste with ¼ cup water.

4 Heat 4 tbsp oil in a kadhai, add boiled onion paste and saute for 7-8 minutes on low heat till dry and oil separates. See that the colour of the onions does not change to brown.

5 Add ginger-garlic paste and stir-fry for a minute.

6 Add dhania powder, pepper powder and salt and mix well.

7 Stir in the pista-green chilli paste and cook for 2 minutes on low heat.

8 Add Sugam Paneer and 1½ cups water & simmer on low heat for 2-3 minutes.

9 Add yogurt, simmer for 1 minute, stirring continuously.

10 Stir in fresh cream, sprinkle garam masala powder and transfer to a serving dish. Sprinkle remaining pistachio nuts and some cream. Serve hot.

Sugam Paneer Makhani

Picture on facing page   *Serves 4*

METHOD

1 Soak kaju in a little warm water for 10-15 minutes.

2 Drain kaju. Grind in a mixer to a very smooth paste using about 2 tbsp water.

3 Boil tomatoes in ½ cup water. Simmer for 4-5 minutes on low heat till tomatoes turn soft. Remove from heat and cool. Grind the tomatoes along with the water to a smooth puree.

4 Heat oil and butter in a kadhai. Add ginger-garlic paste. Mix.

5 When paste starts to change colour add the above tomato puree and cook till dry.

6 Add kasoori methi & tomato ketchup.

7 Add masalas - dhania powder, garam masala, salt and red chilli powder. Mix well for a few seconds. Cook till oil separates.

8 Add cashew paste. Mix well for 2 minutes.

9 Add water. Boil. Simmer on low heat for 4-5 minutes. Reduce heat.

10 Add the Sugam Paneer cubes. Remove from heat. Keep aside to cool for about 5 minutes.

11 Add enough milk to the cold Sugam Paneer masala to get a thick curry, mix gently. (Remember to add milk only after the masala is no longer hot, to prevent the milk from curdling. After adding milk, heat curry on low heat.)

12 Heat on low heat, stirring continuously till just about to boil.

13 Add cream, keeping the heat very low and stirring continuously. Remove from heat immediately and transfer to a serving dish. Swirl 1 tbsp cream over the hot Sugam Paneer in the dish. Serve immediately.

Variation:

For dakshini tadka, heat 1 tbsp oil. Add ½ tsp rai. After 30 seconds add 4-5 curry leaves. Stir. Remove from heat. Add a pinch of red chilli powder and pour over the hot Sugam Paneer makhani in the dish.

Dum Sugam Paneer Kali Mirch

Dum - The Avadh way to flavour the cooked dish. Here the spices are added to the dish at the end of the cooking. The dish is sealed with dough or a very tight fitting lid and kept on very low heat in the oven or on heat, for the Sugam Paneer to absorb the exotic flavour of the spice added. The black peppercorns here lend their flavour to the Sugam Paneer.

Serves 6   *Picture on page 106*

INGREDIENTS

300 gms/10 oz **Sugam Paneer** - cut into 1" cubes
½ cup fresh coriander leaves
¼ cup fresh mint leaves - finely chopped
1 cup yogurt (curd) - beat till smooth
2 tbsp ghee
2 bay leaves (tej patta)
1" stick cinnamon (dalchini)
3-4 green cardamoms (chhoti illaichi)
3-4 cloves (laung)
2 tbsp ground coriander (dhania powder)
1 tsp jeera powder (ground cumin)
1½ tsp salt or to taste

DUM INGREDIENTS
1 level tbsp peppercorns (saboot kali mirch) -
crushed in a spice grinder
½ cup fresh cream, ½ tsp garam masala

PASTE
2-3 green chillies
1" piece ginger - chopped
4-5 flakes garlic
4 onions - sliced and deep fried till golden

2 Grind the fried onions along with garlic, ginger and green chillies with ¼ cup water to a smooth paste. Keep aside onion- garlic paste.

3 Heat ghee in a narrow-mouthed handi or a pan with a well fitting lid.

4 Add tej patta, dalchini, chhoti illaichi and laung. Wait for ½ minute.

METHOD

1 For paste- finely slice the onions. Heat oil in a kadhai and deep fry the sliced onions in hot oil till golden brown. Drain on an absorbent paper napkin and cool.

5 Add onion-garlic paste and saute for 2 minutes on low heat.

6 Reduce heat. Add the beaten yogurt. Mix well.

7 Add dhania powder, jeera powder and salt to taste. Stir for 2 minutes. Add 2 cups water and bring to a boil.

8 Add the Sugam Paneer pieces and mix in the chopped coriander and mint leaves.

9 Stir in the fresh cream and crushed black peppercorns. Sprinkle garam masala.

10 Cover the handi with a tightfitting lid and seal using whole wheat flour (atta dough) or alternately, seal tightly with aluminium foil.

11 Preheat oven to 180°C/350°F. Place sealed handi in the preheated oven or on a tawa on very low heat and cook for 10-15 minutes. Open the handi just before serving and serve immediately.

For more info, visit: www.sugampaneer.com

Shahi Malai Kofta

Just follow the recipe step by step and see how simple it is to prepare this elaborate dish of koftas a creamy whitish gravy.

Picture on facing page   Serves 6

INGREDIENTS

KOFTA
200 gm/7 oz **Sugam Paneer** - grated (2 cups)
1 boiled potato - grated
2 tbsp finely chopped coriander (hara dhania)
½ tsp each of garam masala & red chilli powder
¾ tsp salt, or to taste
2½ tbsp plain flour (maida)

TO COAT
2-3 tbsp plain flour (maida)

GRAVY
3 onions - ground to a paste in a mixer
4 tbsp kaju - soak in ½ cup hot water
4 tbsp yogurt
½ cup malai or cream or ½ cup milk
2 tbsp ghee or butter or 3 tbsp oil
1 tsp garam masala
¾ tsp red chilli powder
a pinch of turmeric (haldi)
1 tbsp dry fenugreek leaves (kasoori methi)
1 tsp salt, or to taste
seeds of 3 green cardamoms (chhoti illaichi) - crushed

METHOD

1 To prepare the koftas, mix grated Sugam Paneer, potatoes, fresh coriander, salt, garam masala, red chilli powder and 2½ tbsp maida. Mix well till smooth. Make 12 balls.

2 Spread 2-3 tbsp maida on a plate. R each ball in maida. Dust to remo excess maida.

3 Heat oil in a kadhai for frying. De fry 1 kofta at a time in medium hot till light brown. Keep fried koftas aside.

4 Soak kaju in ½ cup hot water for minutes. Drain away the water. Gri the softened cashews to a very fine pa with 4 tbsp yogurt in a small grinder. Ke cashew paste aside.

5 For the gravy, heat ghee in a hea bottomed kadhai or a non stick pa Add onion paste. Stir on low heat till it tur transparent and ghee separates and t sides of the kadhai looks glossy because the separated ghee. Do not let the onio turn brown by keeping on high hea (Remember, we are making a white gra and not a brown one!) Add haldi. Stir fo few seconds.

6 Add kaju-yogurt paste. Cook for 2-3 minutes on low heat. Add garam masala, red chilli powder and salt.

7 Add kasoori methi and stir for 2 minutes. Add 1 cup water to make a thick gravy. Boil on low heat for 3-4 minutes. Remove from heat and let it cool.

8 At the time of serving, add powdered chhoti illaichi and cream or milk to the gravy. Add enough milk to get the right consistency of the gravy. Keep on low heat and bring to boil. Add koftas and simmer on low heat for 1 minute. Serve garnished with a swirl of cream, roasted magaz and coriander leaves.

Caution!

Fry only one kofta at a time in hot oil on medium heat. Too many koftas at a time in oil, reduces the temperature of oil. End result...koftas break on frying.

Kali Mirch Sugam Paneer Tukri

Kali Mirch Sugam Paneer Tukri

Serves 4   *Picture on opposite page*

INGREDIENTS

200 gm/6 oz Sugam Paneer - cut into ¼" thick slices
1 tsp peppercorns (saboot kali mirch) - crushed
roughly, 2 tsp butter

GRAVY

3 tbsp oil or ghee, ¼ tsp carom seeds (ajwain)
2-3 flakes garlic - crushed
½ onion - chopped, ½ capsicum - chopped
½ tsp garam masala, 1 tsp dhania powder
½ tsp red chilli powder, ½ tsp salt, or to taste
½ cup ready made tomato puree
1-2 tsp tomato ketchup
½ cup water mixed with 1 tsp cornflour

METHOD

1 Spread softened butter on both sides of Sugam Paneer slices.

2 Sprinkle half of the crushed peppercorns on the Sugam Paneer slices and press well to embed them into the slices. Turn slices and repeat. Cut each piece into 2 triangles.

3 For the gravy, heat oil. Add ajwain. Wait for ½ minute.

4 Add garlic. Let garlic change colour.

5 Add onion. Stir till transparent on low heat for 1 minute.

6 Add masalas - garam masala, dhania powder, red chilli powder and salt. Mix well for ½ minute. Add capsicum.

7 Add tomato puree. Cook till dry, for about 2-3 minutes.

8 Add water and cornflour. Add tomato ketchup. Simmer on low heat for 5 minutes till slightly thick. Keep aside.

9 To serve, heat a nonstick tawa or an oven. Brown Sugam Paneer pieces on the pan or on the hot grill of the oven. Cook till well heated and light brown on both sides.

10 Heat gravy, put some at the base of the dish. Arrange the pieces of Sugam Paneer on top. Sprinkle some gravy on it if desired.

Baby Corn and Sugam Paneer Korma

Korma is a rich fragrant sauce with a yogurt-tomato base. A bay leaf dropped in hot oil, imparts a lovely flavour to the curry.

Picture on facing page   *Serves 8-10*

INGREDIENTS

100 gm/4 oz Sugam Paneer - cut into 1" cubes
100 gm/ 4 oz baby corns - ½" slices
4 tbsp oil
1 bay leaf (tej patta)
2-3 flakes garlic - crushed
1 large onion - ground to a paste (½ cup)
¾ tsp tandoori masala
¼ tsp sugar (optional)
coriander leaves for garnishing

YOGURT-TOMATO PASTE
½ cup yogurt
1 big tomato - chopped (¾ cup)
1-2 green chillies, 2 tbsp cashews (kaju)
a pinch of turmeric
½ tsp salt, or to taste
½ tsp red chilli powder, ½ tsp garam masala

METHOD

1 Grind all ingredients of the yogurt-tomato paste together to a smooth paste. Check that the cashews get ground properly. Keep the paste aside.

2 Heat oil. Reduce heat. Add bay leaf and garlic. Let garlic turn light brown. Add onion paste and stir till golden.

3 Add the yogurt-tomato paste and stir fry for 8-10 minutes on medium heat till dry and oil separates. Add about 1 cup of water. Bring to a boil.

4 Add tandoori masala. Add sugar, if the curry tastes sour (if the yogurt added is sour, sugar needs to be added). Simmer curry for 7-8 minutes till oil surfaces. Remove from heat.

5 Fry the Sugam Paneer and the baby corns to a golden colour in two separate batches.

5

6 Add fried Sugam Paneer and baby corns to the gravy. Simmer for 3-4 minutes. Transfer to a serving dish and garnish with a few whole coriander leaves. Serve hot with rice or bread.

Note: If you do not want to fry the baby corns, add raw slices to the curry and simmer in it till they get cooked. Sugam Paneer can also be added without frying.

113

Pepper Sugam Paneer Chettinad

The fiery, delicious, brown curry of Chettinad - a place in South India.

Picture on facing page   Serves 4-6

INGREDIENTS

250 gm/8 oz Sugam Paneer **- cut into**
1½" pieces and fried till golden
1 tbsp poppy seeds (khus khus)
2 tbsp cashewnuts (kaju)
4 tbsp oil
1 large onion - finely chopped
3 tomatoes - chopped
10-12 curry patta
1½ tsp salt, or to taste, ½ tsp haldi
1 tsp chilli powder
1" piece ginger, 8-10 flakes garlic
1 tbsp lemon juice or to taste

CHETTINAD MASALA (ROASTED & GROUND)
½ cup freshly grated coconut (remove brown
skin before grating)
1 tsp coriander seeds (saboot dhania)
1" cinnamon stick (dalchini)
½ tsp cumin seeds (jeera)
1 tsp fennel (saunf)
2-3 dry, whole red chillies
seeds of 3 green cardamoms (chhoti illaichi)
2-3 cloves (laung)

METHOD

1   Soak khus khus and cashewnuts in a little warm water for 10-15 minutes.

2   Heat 1 tbsp oil in a kadhai or tawa. Add all ingredients of the chettinad masala. Stir-fry for 3-4 minutes till fragrant and golden. Remove from heat.

3 Drain the khus-khus and cashews. Grind together the roasted masala with the drained khus-khus, cashewnuts, ginger and garlic in a mixer blender to a very smooth paste using about ½ cup water.

4 Heat oil in a kadhai and add the chopped onions. Fry till golden.

5 Add the ground paste and curry leaves. Saute for ½ a minute.

6 Add the chopped tomatoes, salt, haldi and chilli powder. Cook for about 10 minutes on medium heat, stirring in between till tomatoes are well blended.

7 Add lemon juice and 1½ cups of water. Boil. Simmer for 5-7 minutes. If you desire a thinner gravy, add some more water and bring to a boil 3-4 times.

8 Add fried Sugam Paneer and boil. Simmer for 2-3 minutes. Garnish with coriander and some freshly ground pepper.

Paalak Sugam Paneer

A quick and tasty way of making this evergreen spinach dish.

Picture on facing page   Serves 4

INGREDIENTS

**500 gm/1 lb spinach (paalak), choose a bundle
with smaller leaves, 3 tbsp oil
1 brown cardamom (moti illaichi)
2-3 cloves (laung)
3-4 peppercorns (saboot kali mirch)
3 onions - chopped
1" piece ginger - chopped
4-6 flakes garlic - chopped
1 green chilli - chopped
1 tbsp dried fenugreek leaves (kasoori methi)
¾ tsp garam masala, ½ tsp red chilli powder
¼ tsp amchoor, 1¼ tsp salt, or to taste
2 tomatoes - chopped
100 gms/4 oz Sugam Paneer - cut into 1" cubes
1 cup milk**

**BAGHAR (TEMPERING)
1 tbsp ghee or butter
1" piece ginger - cut into thin long pieces
1 green chilli - slit into long pieces
½ tsp red chilli powder**

METHOD

1 Break paalak leaves from the stem. Discard stems. Wash in plenty of water. Keep aside to drain.

2 Heat oil in a kadhai. Add moti illaichi, laung and saboot kali mirch.

3 Add chopped onions and cook till light brown.

4 Add ginger, garlic and green chillies. Stir on low heat for 1 minute. Add kasoori methi.

5 Add garam masala, red chilli powder, amchoor and salt. Stir on low heat for 1 minute.

6 Add chopped tomatoes. Cook for 3-4 minutes, till well blended.

7 Add spinach and cook uncovered for 10-12 minutes on low heat. Remove from heat. Cool.

8   Blend the cooled mixture along with ½ cup water, just for a few seconds, to a coarse paste. Do not grind it too finely.

9   Add 1 cup milk & Sugam Paneer pieces to the spinach paste. Cook on low heat for 2-3 minutes till Sugam Paneer turns soft. Check salt and remove from heat. Transfer to a serving dish.

10   Heat 1 tbsp ghee or butter. Add ginger and green chilli. Remove from heat. Add red chilli powder and pour oil on the hot paalak. Mix lightly. Serve.

Manzil-e-Sugam Paneer

Picture on facing page   Serves 8

2 Heat 2 tbsp oil. Reduce heat. Add garlic and stir till it just starts to change colour. Add 6 tbsp ready-made tomato puree. Add fresh puree also. Cook till oil separates, for about 8-10 minutes on medium heat. Let it cool.

3 Mix in milk to get a thin gravy. Add salt and pepper to taste and keep the gravy aside.

METHOD

1 To prepare the sauce, boil chopped tomatoes and saunf in ½ cup water. Keep on low heat for 4-5 minutes till soft. Remove from heat, cool completely. Grind in a mixer till smooth. Strain puree. Discard the skin. Keep fresh tomato puree aside.

4 Cut Sugam Paneer into 3 equal pieces lengthwise, getting full pieces of about ½" thick. Do not make them too thick. Sprinkle salt, red chilli powder, haldi and chat masala on both sides of each slice of Sugam Paneer. Saute in 2 tbsp oil in a nonstick pan, changing sides carefully, till golden on both sides.

7 Spread ½ of the carrot filling on it. Press another piece of Sugam Paneer on it. Spread 2-3 tbsp gravy on it.

8 Again put the filling on it. Cover with the last piece of Sugam Paneer. Press.

9 Pour the gravy all over the Sugam Paneer to cover the top and the sides completely. Grate cheese on top. Garnish with tomatoes and capsicum. Sprinkle some pepper.

5 In a shallow rectangular serving dish, put 2-3 tbsp of the prepared tomato gravy.

6 Place a Sugam Paneer slab on the sauce. Spread some gravy on it.

10 If using a microwave, cover loosely with a cling film and micro high for 2 minutes. If using an ordinary oven, cover loosely with aluminium foil and heat for 8-10 minutes in a moderately hot oven at 180°C/350°F till hot.

Butter Sugam Paneer Masala

Onion and capsicum rings with Sugam Paneer in a red makhani gravy.

Picture on facing page   *Serves 4-5*

INGREDIENTS

250 gms/8 oz **Sugam Paneer** - cut into triangles
4 big (250 gms/8 oz) tomatoes - pureed
2 tsp kasoori methi (dry fenugreek leaves)
½ cup (100 ml/3 fluid oz) milk
¾ tsp roasted cumin seeds (bhuna jeera)
powder
1 tsp red chilli powder, ½ tsp garam masala
1½ tsp salt, or to taste, ¼ - ½ tsp sugar
1 green chilli - slit lengthwise
1 big capsicum - cut into rings
2 onions - cut into thin rings
2 tbsp butter
few drops orange food colour

PASTE
2 onions - chopped
1" piece ginger - chopped
6-7 flakes garlic

METHOD

1 Cut capsicum and onion into rings. Keep aside.

2 Grind onions, ginger and garlic together to a paste.

3 Grind tomatoes to a puree.

120

4 Heat 5 tbsp oil in a kadhai, add onion paste in oil, till golden (on the lighter side). Do not make it brown.

5 Add tomatoes. Cook for 10-15 minutes on low heat till oil separates. Add bhuna jeera powder, red chilli powder, garam masala, salt and sugar.

6 Add enough water, about 1½ cups. Cook for another 10-12 minutes till the oil separates and the gravy dries up to a thick masala gravy.

7 Add kasoori methi and milk. Cook on low heat for 2 minutes, stirring continuously. Remove from heat.

8 Heat butter in a clean kadhai, add green chillies, capsicum and onions. Saute for 2-3 minutes.

9 Add these vegetables, Sugam Paneer and food colour to the prepared gravy.

10 Return to heat, cook for another 2-3 minutes, stirring continuously. Serve hot.

Dum Aloo

Sugam Paneer stuffed aloos in a delicious subtle Kashmiri gravy. Must give it a try!

Serves 4-6   *Picture on opposite page*

POTATOES
4 medium round potatoes, 3 tbsp maida, oil for frying

FILLING
100 gm/4 oz Sugam Paneer - grated
1 small onion - finely chopped
1 green chilli - chopped finely
4-5 cashewnuts (kajus) - chopped
8-10 raisins (kishmish)- chopped
1 tbsp oil, salt to taste

GRAVY
1 tej patta, 1 tsp royal cumin (shah jeera)
4 tbsp very finely grated Sugam Khoa
1½ tbsp dry fenugreek leaves (kasoori methi)
1½ tsp salt or to taste, ½ tsp garam masala
2 blades of star anise (chakri phool) - crushed

ONION PASTE
1 onion, 2 cloves (laung)
¾" piece of ginger, 4-5 flakes of garlic
seeds of 2 green cardamom (chhoti illaichi)
seeds of 2 black cardamom (moti illaichi)
1" stick cinnamon (dalchini)

TOMATO PASTE
4 tomatoes - boiled in hot water for
3-4 minutes and peeled
¼ tsp jaiphal, ¼ tsp javitri, 2 dry, red chillies
2½ tbsp cashewnuts (kaju)
2 tbsp poppy seeds (khus-khus)

2 Scoop out the inner portion of the potato with a scooper or a knife. Leave a wall of ¼" all around the potato.

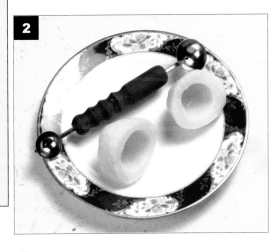

METHOD

1 Peel and wash the potatoes. Prick with a fork. Cut into two pieces, widthwise.

3 Keep the potatoes in salted water for 15 minutes. Strain and pat dry.

4 Heat oil and deep fry all potatoes together till they get cooked properly and are golden brown in colour. Take out 1 piece from oil and check to see if cooked. If done, then remove all pieces from the kadhai on paper napkins. Keep aside till serving time.

5 For filling, heat 1 tbsp oil, add onion and green chilli. Cook till onion turns light golden.

6 Add kaju and kishmish. Cook for 1 minute.

7 Add grated Sugam Paneer and salt. Cook for a few seconds. Remove from heat and cool.

8 Fill potatoes with prepared filling. Press to level it.

9 Spread maida in a flat plate. Invert the potato with the filling side down on the maida.

10 Heat 2 tbsp oil in a pan, put potatoes with the filling side down in oil. Fry on medium heat till maida forms a crisp coating over filling. Remove from heat.

11 Grind all the ingredients of onion paste to a smooth paste. Keep aside.

12 Boil tomatoes in water for 3-4 minutes. Peel. Grind all the ingredients of tomato paste to a smooth paste. Keep aside.

13 For gravy - heat 3 tbsp oil, add tej patta and shah jeera, wait for a minute.

14 Add onion paste. Cook for 2-3 minutes till golden brown.

15 Add tomato paste. Stir for 8-10 minutes or till dry.

16 Add Sugam Khoa, kasoori methi, salt, garam masala and crushed blades of star anise. Cook for 2 minutes, stirring. Add ¾ cup of water. Boil. Simmer for 3 minutes. Remove from heat and keep aside till serving time.

17 At serving time, add 1 cup milk and boil on low heat.

18 Add fried potatoes. Keep on heat for 2-3 minutes. Serve hot.

CHINESE
&
THAI

Veggies in Szechwan Sauce

Picture on facing page   *Serves 4*

INGREDIENTS

**100 gms/4 oz Sugam Paneer - cut into
¼" thick triangular pieces - sprinkled with
¼ tsp salt and white pepper & 1 tbsp cornflour
4-5 florets of broccoli or cauliflower
4-6 babycorns - cut into 2 pieces diagonally
1 carrot - sliced very diagonally and then cut
into 2 pieces, 6-8 leaves of bokchoy or spinach
3-4 dry mushrooms
1 capsicum - cut into 1" pieces
2 tbsp bamboo shoots (tinned) - cut into thin
diagonal slices**

SZECHWAN SAUCE

**4 tbsp oil, 1 onion- cut into 1" pieces
2 laung (cloves) - crushed
3 tbsp ready-made tomato puree
2 tbsp tomato ketchup
1 tsp red chilli sauce, 2 tsp soya sauce
¼ tsp pepper, ½ tsp salt or to taste
1 tsp sugar, or to taste
¼ tsp ajinomoto (optional)
1½ cups water mixed with 2 seasoning stock
vegetable stock or cubes
3 tbsp cornflour mixed with ½ cup water**

PASTE

**1 tbsp chopped garlic, 1 tsp vinegar
2 dry, red chillies - break into bits & remove
some seeds**

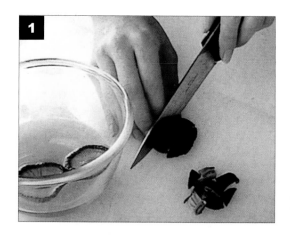

2 If using bokchoy or spinach, remove any discoloured leaves. Tear into two pieces.

METHOD

1 If using dry mushrooms, put them in a pan. Cover with water. Boil. Simmer for 2 minutes. Remove from heat. Keep aside for 10 minutes. Wash several times. Break off any hard stem portion and discard. Wash several times scrubbing well, to clean the hidden dirt. Cut into pieces.

3 Boil 4-5 cups water with 1 tsp salt. Remove from heat. Add broccoli or cauliflower, baby corns, carrots and bokchoy or spinach. Leave veggies in hot water for 1-2 minutes and strain. Refresh in cold water and keep aside till serving time.

4 Roughly grind all ingredients written under paste in a small grinder.

5 Heat 4 tbsp oil in a pan. Shallow fry the Sugam Paneer till golden. Remove Sugam Paneer from pan.

6 To prepare the sauce, heat 2 tbsp oil again in the same pan. Remove from heat. Add garlic-red chilli paste. Stir.

7 Add onion. Saute for 1 minute. Shut off the heat. Add laung, tomato puree, ketchup, red chilli sauce, Soya sauce, pepper, salt, sugar and ajinomoto.

8 Return to heat and cook for 1 minute on low heat.

9 Add stock or water mixed with seasoning cubes. Bring to a boil.

10 Add cornflour paste, stirring all the time. Cook for 2 minutes on low heat. Add bamboo shoots. Remove from heat. Keep aside till serving time.

11 To serve, heat the sauce. Add the soaked mushrooms, Sugam Paneer, blanched vegetables and capsicum. Bring to a boil and simmer for 1 minute. Serve.

Sugam Paneer in Hot Garlic Sauce

Picture on facing page   Serves 3-4

Picture on facing page

INGREDIENTS

150 gm/5 oz Sugam Paneer
2 tbsp plain flour (maida), ¼ cup cornflour
¼ tsp each of pepper & salt
¼ tsp ajinomoto (optional), 4 tbsp water

GARLIC SAUCE
15 flakes garlic - minced (2 tbsp)
1 tbsp oil, 2 tbsp tomato ketchup
4 tbsp tomato puree
1 tsp soya sauce
½ tsp white pepper, ½ tsp salt, or to taste
a pinch of sugar, ¼ tsp ajinomoto (optional)
¾ cup water
1 tbsp cornflour mixed with ¼ cup water
1 spring onion greens - finely chopped (1 tbsp)
for garnishing

METHOD

1 To prepare the sauce, peel and chop the garlic very finely to get minced garlic.

2 Heat 1 tbsp oil and add the garlic on low heat. Stir.

3 Reduce heat. Add tomato ketchup, tomato puree, soya sauce, pepper and salt. Cook for 1 minute.

4 Add sugar and ajinomoto.

5 Add water. Bring to a boil. Simmer for 2 minutes.

6 Add cornflour paste, stirring all the time, until the sauce thickens. Remove from heat. Keep sauce aside.

7 Cut Sugam Paneer into ¾"-1" pieces.

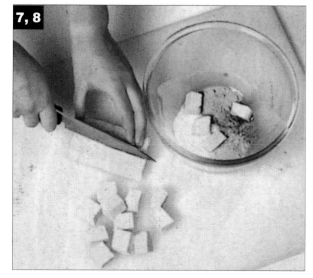

7, 8

10 At the time of serving, heat sauce. Put the fried Sugam Paneer pieces and boil for 1-2 minutes till Sugam Paneer turns soft. Transfer to a serving dish.

11 Garnish with spring onion greens or chopped capsicum and serve with fried rice.

8 Mix cornflour, plain flour, salt, pepper, ajinomoto, water and Sugam Paneer.

9 Deep fry Sugam Paneer to a golden colour.

9

Red Thai Curry

Serves 4-6

Picture on page 132

INGREDIENTS

RED CURRY PASTE

4 Kashmiri dry, red chillies - soaked in ½ cup
warm water for 10 minutes
½ onion - chopped
8-10 flakes garlic - peeled
½" piece ginger - sliced
1 stalk lemon grass (use only the lower part) or
rind of 1 lemon (see note)
1½ tsp coriander seeds (dhania saboot)
1 tsp cumin (jeera)
6 peppercorns (saboot kali mirch)
1 tsp salt, 1 tbsp lemon juice

SUGAM PANEER & VEGETABLES

200 gm/6 oz Sugam Paneer - cut into 1" pieces
1 small carrot - peeled and cut into fours
lengthwise and then into 1" pieces
4 french beans - threaded & cut into 1" length
6-8 baby corns - cut lengthwise into 2 pieces
½ of a small broccoli or ½ of a small
cauliflower - cut into medium florets (1 cup)
¼ cup chopped bamboo shoots, optional

OTHER INGREDIENTS

3 cups coconut milk, fresh or ready made
10-12 basil leaves
½ tsp soya sauce, salt to taste
½ tsp brown sugar or regular sugar

2 Extract 2 cups coconut milk by soaking grated coconut in 1 cup of hot water. Blend and then strain. Keep milk aside. Add more hot water to the left over coconut and blend to get 3 cups of coconut milk in all.

3 Heat 3 tbsp oil, add red curry paste. Fry for 2 minutes on low heat.

METHOD

1 Grind all the ingredients of the red curry paste along with the water in which the chillies were soaked, to a paste.

4 Add ¼ cup of coconut milk. Add all vegetables and stir fry for 2-3 minutes.

6 Add Sugam Paneer, basil leaves, salt and sugar to taste. Boil for 2-3 minutes. Serve hot with steamed rice.

5 Add the rest of the coconut milk and soya sauce. Simmer on low heat for 5-7 minutes till vegetables turn tender.

About Lemon Grass

Discard the bottom 1" of the stalk and peel some of the outer leaves. Chop stalk and use it in curry pastes. The upper grass like portion is not edible and is added to dishes like soups, rice and curries to flavour them but removed from the dish before serving. Lemon grass will keep well for about 1-2 weeks in the fridge. Use 1-2 stalks per dish.

Note: For lemon rind, wash & grate 1 lemon with the peel gently on the grater to get lemon rind. Do not apply pressure and see that the white pith beneath the lemon peel is not grated along with the yellow rind. The white pith is bitter!

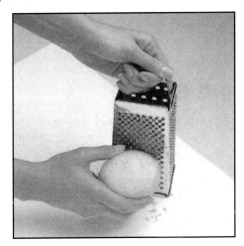

Helpful Hint

Red curry paste can be made extra & stored in an airtight box, for upto 1 month. For a bright red paste, use dry, broad big Kashmiri chillies preferably & not usual thin long ones.

Stir fried Snow Peas/Beans

Use any combination of vegetables that you have on hand or just Sugam Paneer and spring onions to make this quick stir-fry.

Picture on facing page   *Serves 4*

INGREDIENTS

200 gms/7 oz snow peas or french beans
50-75 gm/2 oz Sugam Paneer - cut into thin,
2" long pieces
1 onion, 4 tbsp oil
1½" piece ginger - cut into jullienes or
thin match sticks (1½ tbsp)
3-4 green chillies - shredded (cut into thin
pieces lengthwise)

OTHER INGREDIENTS

1½ tbsp soya sauce, 2½ tbsp tomato ketchup
1 tbsp vinegar, 1 tsp red chilli sauce
2 tbsp sherry or wine (optional)
1½ tbsp worcester sauce
½ tsp salt, ¼ tsp pepper, or to taste
½ tsp ajinomoto (optional)
1 tbsp dry bread crumbs, optional

SNOW PEAS/MANGETOUT:
They belong to the
pea family and are
used in cooking just
like we use French
beans. Whole pod
is edible. Snap off the stem
end of pea pod and pull the
thread.

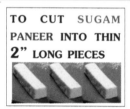

TO CUT SUGAM
PANEER INTO THIN
2" LONG PIECES

METHOD

1 Remove strings/threads from snow peas or beans.

2 If using snow peas, keep whole. If using french beans, cut each into 1½-2" pieces. Boil 4-5 cups water with 1 tsp salt and 1 tsp sugar. Add beans or snowpeas and boil for 1-2 minutes. Strain.

134

3 Peel onion. Cut into half and then cut widthwise to get half rings, which when opened become thin long strips and you get shredded onion.

4 Heat 4 tbsp oil in pan. Add onion, cook till golden.

5 Add ginger jullienes and green chillies. Stir fry for 1-2 minutes till ginger turns golden.

6 Add snow peas or beans and stir fry for 3-4 minutes till vegetable turns crisp-tender. Keep the vegetable spread out in the pan while stir frying.

7 Reduce heat. Add soya sauce, tomato ketchup, vinegar, red chilli sauce, sherry, worcester sauce, salt, pepper and ajinomoto.

8 Add Sugam Paneer and mix well.

9 Add bread crumbs. Stir fry on low heat for 2 minutes till the vegetable blends well with the sauces. Serve hot.

Green Thai Sugam Paneer Curry with Aubergines

Picture on facing page   *Serves 4*

INGREDIENTS

200 gms/6 oz Sugam Paneer
2-3 small aubergines (brinjals/baingan) -
peeled & cut into thin slices and sprinkled
with ¼ tsp salt
2½ cups ready-made coconut milk
½ tsp dried basil
¾ tsp salt, 1 tsp sugar or gur
2 tbsp basil or chopped coriander leaves
2-3 green or red chillies - slit long
for garnishing

GREEN CURRY PASTE
6-7 green chillies
½ onion - chopped
1 tbsp chopped garlic
½" piece ginger - chopped
1 stick lemon grass - cut into pieces, see note
2-3 lemon leaves or
½ tsp lemon rind (see note)
½ cup basil leaves or coriander leaves
½ tsp salt, 1 tbsp lemon juice
1 tbsp coriander seeds (saboot dhania)
15 peppercorns (saboot kali mirch)
1 tbsp cumin seeds (jeera) - roasted on a tawa

METHOD

1 For the green curry paste, dry roast coriander seeds and cumin seeds for 2 minutes on a tawa till fragrant but not brown. Put all other ingredients of the curry paste and the roasted seeds in a grinder and grind to a fine paste, using a little water.

2 Heat oil in a kadhai. Add green curry paste. Fry for 2-3 minutes.

3 Add 1 cup coconut milk. Simmer on low heat for 5-7 minutes.

4 Add dry basil, salt, sugar, brinjals and the rest of coconut milk. Boil. Cover and cook on low heat for about 5 minutes or till brinjals are well cooked.

5 Add Sugam Paneer. Bring to a boil 2-3 times.

6 Garnish with sliced red or green chillies (long thin slices), basil leaves.

7 Serve hot with boiled/steamed rice.

CONTINENTAL

Baked Corn with Sugam Paneer

Sugam Paneer is marinated in mustard dressing and then baked with corn in a mustard sauce.

Picture on facing page   *Serves 2-3*

INGREDIENTS

200 gm/6 oz Sugam Paneer - cut into ½" pieces
½ cup chopped green capsicum
1 cup tinned corn kernels
30 whole, small spinach leaves - remove stem
and tear each leaf into half
6 tbsp grated cheese, preferably
mozzarella cheese or pizza cheese
3 tbsp chopped walnuts (akhrot)

MARINADE
1 tsp mustard paste
1 tsp lemon juice
¼ tsp freshly ground peppercorns (saboot kali
mirch), ½ tsp salt

MUSTARD SAUCE
2 tbsp butter
1 small onion - sliced finely
2 tbsp plain flour (maida)
2 cups milk, 1 tsp salt
¾ tsp pepper
½ tsp dried basil or 2 tbsp fresh basil leaves
2 tsp mustard paste

3 Add flour and stir on low heat for a minute.

METHOD

1 Marinate Sugam Paneer with mustard paste, lemon juice, salt and pepper. Mix well. Keep aside.

2 To make the mustard sauce, melt butter in a kadhai or pan. Add onions and stir till soft.

4 Add capsicum and corn. Stir for ½ minute.

5 Add milk, stirring continuously and cook till it coats the back of a spoon.

6 Add basil, salt, pepper and mustard paste. Remove from heat. Keep sauce aside.

7 Arrange spinach leaves overlapping slightly in a small, greased borosil dish.

8 Arrange the Sugam Paneer over the spinach leaves.

9 Pour the prepared mustard sauce over it.

10 Arrange spinach overlapping slightly on the sauce.

11 Mix grated cheese and walnuts and sprinkle on top. Bake at 180°C/ 350°F for 15 minutes till cheese melts.

Sugam Paneer & Veg Sizzler

Picture on facing page   Serves 2

Picture on facing page

INGREDIENTS

100 gms/4 oz Sugam Paneer - cut into 1" pieces
6 mushrooms - cut into halves
1 small onion - sliced
1 carrot - cut into small cubes and boiled
½ capsicum - cut into thin long pieces
1 slice of tinned pineapple - cut into small pieces
½ tsp salt and ½ tsp freshly crushed pepper, or to taste

SAUCE
6-7 flakes garlic - crushed, **2 tbsp oil**
2 green chillies - deseeded & chopped finely
½ tbsp soya sauce
a few drops tabasco sauce
1 tbsp red chilli sauce, 3 tbsp tomato ketchup
1 tbsp vinegar, ¼ tsp pepper and ½ tsp salt, or to taste
2 level tbsp cornflour dissolved in 1½ cups water

TO SERVE
2 tbsp butter, a sizzler plate
rice boiled with salt and lemon juice

2 Add capsicum, pineapple and Sugam Paneer. Add salt and freshly crushed pepper. Cook for 1 minute. Remove all vegetables and Sugam Paneer from the kadhai and keep aside.

3 To prepare the sauce, heat 2 tbsp oil in a clean kadhai. Reduce heat. Add garlic & green chillies. Stir for a few seconds on low heat till garlic just changes colour.

METHOD

1 Heat 2 tbsp oil in a nonstick pan or kadhai. Add mushrooms. Saute till light brown and dry. Add onion. Saute for 2 minutes. Add carrots. Stir for 1-2 minutes.

4 Remove from heat. Add all sauces and vinegar. Cook on slow heat for a few seconds. Add salt and pepper to taste. Add cornflour paste, stirring continuously till a sauce is ready. Add vegetables and Sugam Paneer. Cook for 1 minute on low heat.

5 To serve, remove the iron sizzler plate from the wooden base. Heat the iron plate by keeping it directly on the heat. Reduce heat and let the iron plate be on heat while it is being filled. Put 2-3 tbsp water in the wooden base and scatter 1 tbsp butter cut into pieces on the wooden base. Keep wooden base aside.

6 When the iron plate is heated, scatter 1 tbsp butter here and there. Place 2-3 cabbage leaves on the plate and arrange rice on it. Leave on slow heat for 2 minutes for the rice to get heated. Put the hot vegetables in sauce in the centre portion of the rice. When the hot sauce falls on the hot plate, it sizzles. With the help of a firm pair of tongs (sansi), place the iron plate on the wooden tray. Serve sizzling hot.

Stuffed Cheese Steaks

Picture on facing page   Serves 4

INGREDIENTS

500 gm/1 lb **Sugam Paneer** - cut into
1½"x 2" pieces of 1" thickness

FILLING
6-7 french beans - cut into paper thin slices
¼ cup finely grated carrot (½ carrot)
¼ tsp salt, ¼ tsp oregano
a pinch of pepper, or to taste
½ cube cheese - grated finely (2 tbsp)
½ tbsp butter, 1 tbsp grated onion (½ onion)

PEPPER SAUCE
2 tsp chopped garlic, ½ tsp ginger paste
½ tsp peppercorns (saboot kali mirch) - crushed
4 peppercorns (saboot kali mirch)
½-1 tsp soya sauce, 1 tbsp tomato ketchup
a pinch of ajinomoto, 1 tsp vinegar
1½ tbsp cornflour, 2 tbsp butter or oil
1½ cups hot water mixed with 1 vegetable-
seasoning cube

BATTER
3 tbsp plain flour (maida)
¼ cup plus 1 tbsp milk
2 pinches turmeric (haldi), ¼ tsp salt
¼ tsp red chilli powder
2 tbsp very finely grated cheese

2   For the filling, heat butter. Add onion. Stir fry for 2 minutes. Add beans. Cook covered for 3 minutes on low heat till soft. Add carrots, salt, oregano and pepper stir for 1 minute. Remove from heat. Add cheese. Keep aside to cool.

3   Take a piece of Sugam Paneer. Spread 1 tsp of the filling on it. Press another piece of Sugam Paneer on it. Turn and press the other side also to join properly. Keep aside.

METHOD

1   Cut Sugam Paneer into thick, big rectangular pieces. Divide each piece into 2 pieces. Sprinkle salt and freshly ground pepper on both sides on each piece and keep aside.

4 For the batter, mix all ingredients of the batter together. Keep aside.

5 For pepper sauce, mix cornflour in ½ cup water. Keep aside the cornflour paste.

6 Heat butter, reduce heat & add garlic, ginger paste, crushed peppercorns & whole peppercorns. Cook till garlic changes colour. Add soya sauce, tomato ketchup, ajinomoto & vinegar. Add hot water mixed with seasoning cube. Boil.

7 Add cornflour paste. Cook stirring continuously till sauce thickens slightly. Remove from heat. Do not overcook the sauce; otherwise it gets very thick.

8 At serving time heat ½ tbsp butter in a nonstick pan on medium heat. Dip the stuffed steak in the prepared batter to coat all sides and put in the pan. Cook 4 pieces at a time. Reduce heat after 2 minutes when the edges start changing colour. Turn the side gently with a flat spoon. Cook till browned on both sides.

9 Top steaks with some pepper sauce & serve the remaining sauce separately.

Iman Binaldey

Picture on facing page   Serves 6

INGREDIENTS

100 gm/4 oz Sugam Paneer - cut into ¼" pieces
2 cups kabuli channa (chick peas) - soaked
overnight, a pinch of mitha soda
¼ of red, yellow or green capsicum,
for garnish

WHITE SAUCE
2½ tbsp butter, 1 onion - finely chopped
2½ tbsp plain flour (maida), 2 cups milk
1 tsp salt and ¼ tsp pepper, or to taste
½ cup grated cheddar cheese

TOMATO SAUCE
1 onion - cut into thin slices
½ kg tomatoes - blended to a puree in a mixer
3 tbsp ready-made tomato puree
2 tbsp tomato sauce
4 flakes garlic - crushed
¼ cup basil or coriander leaves
1 tsp dried oregano
½ tsp chilli powder
½ tsp sugar, 1 tsp salt, or to taste

METHOD

1 To boil channas, drain the water from the channas. Add 4 cups water, 1½ tsp salt and a pinch of mitha soda. Pressure cook to give one whistle. Keep on low heat for about 10 minutes. Remove from heat. Keep aside.

2 To prepare the white sauce, melt the butter in a heavy bottomed pan or a kadhai. Add onion and stir till it just changes colour. Sprinkle flour and cook on low heat for 1 minute without browning, stirring throughout. Remove from heat and gradually add the milk. Mix until well blended. Return to heat and cook slowly for about 2 minutes on low heat, stirring throughout until the sauce thickens and coats the spoon well. Remove from heat. Add cheese, salt and pepper. Mix well.

146

3 For the tomato sauce, heat 2 tbsp oil and fry the onion for 2-3 minutes till it slightly changes colour. Add the fresh tomato puree, ready made tomato puree, tomato sauce, garlic and basil leaves. Add 1 tsp oregano, ½ tsp chilli powder, ½ tsp sugar and 1 tsp salt. Boil for 10 minutes on low heat till the juice from the tomatoes evaporates and it turns slightly thick.

4 Add the boiled channas along with the water. Cook till the extra water evaporates and the tomato masala coats the channas slightly. Add Sugam Paneer. Mix. Check salt etc. and remove from heat.

5 In a oven proof dish, spread 4 tbsp white sauce at the base.

6 Spread channas on white sauce, filling the dish.

7 Spread the remaining white sauce with a tbsp on channas, leaving gaps of 2" in between. This way you get red and white strips. Start from the corner, dropping a few tbsp of white sauce in a row, leave a gap and then drop some white sauce in a row. This way you get a red and white striped look.

8 Arrange a few coloured capsicum slices diagonally on the white row. Bake in a preheated oven for 20 minutes at 180°C/350°F. Serve hot.

Crepes Florentine

The word "florentine' suggests the presence of spinach in the dish. Here are pancakes filled with spinach and smothered with some sauce.

Serves 8　　　　　　　　　　*Picture on page 150*

INGREDIENTS

10-12 PANCAKES
1 cup flour (maida)
1 tsp salt, ½ tsp pepper
¼ tsp soda-bi-carb (mitha soda)
1¾ cups milk, approx.

WHITE SAUCE
2 tbsp butter - softened, 2 tbsp flour (maida)
2 cups milk
¾ tsp salt and ½ tsp pepper, or to taste

FILLING
500 gm/1lb spinach (palak) - finely chopped (4-5 cups)
200 gm/8 oz mushrooms
2 tbsp butter, 2 onions - chopped finely
salt and pepper to taste
1 cup grated Sugam Paneer
2 tbsp thick cream

OTHER INGREDIENTS
50 gm/2 oz mozzarella or pizza cheese - grated (½ cup)
1 tomato - cut into slices & parsley or mint sprigs for garnishing

3 Heat a non stick pan. Smear 1 tsp oil in the centre. Remove pan from heat and pour 1 ladle (karchhi) of batter.

METHOD

1 To prepare the pancakes, sift maida, salt, pepper and soda-bi-carb together.

2 Add milk gradually. Mix well with a whisk. Add enough milk to get a thin pouring consistency.

4 Tilt the pan to spread the batter very thinly. Return to heat and cook till the under side gets done. Remove pancake from pan. (Cook only one side, do not turn the pancake). Make thin, medium size (6" diameter) pancakes. Similarly make all the pancakes and keep aside.

5 To prepare the white sauce, melt butter and add flour. Stir for a minute on low heat. Add milk, stirring continuously. Add salt and pepper to taste. Cook till it starts to coat the spoon. Remove from heat. Do not make it too thick.

6 For the filling, remove the hard stems of the spinach and chop finely. Use about 4-5 cups chopped spinach.

7 Cut 2-3 mushrooms into neat paper thin slices for garnishing and keep aside. Chop the rest of the mushrooms into small pieces.

8 Heat butter in a large pan or kadhai. Add onion. Saute for 1 minute. Add the chopped mushrooms. Add ½ tsp salt and ¼ tsp pepper and cook for 3-4 minutes till all the juices drawn from mushrooms evaporate.

9 Add the spinach. Cook till dry. Remove from heat. Let it come to room temperature.

10 Add the Sugam Paneer and cream. Mix well. Add a little salt and red chilli powder to taste.

11 To assemble, divide filling into 10-12 parts or heaps, according to the number of pancakes prepared. Take a pancake. Spread half of the one part (heap) of the filling on ½ of the pancake and fold over to get a semi circle. Now, spread the remaining half of the same part of the filling (heap) on the semi circle and fold again into half to get a triangle. Repeat this with all pancakes.

12 Take a shallow rectangular oven proof dish. Spread 1/3 of the white sauce. Arrange the pancakes, slightly overlapping each other.

13 Leaving ½" inch from both sides, pour the remaining white sauce on the pancakes on the centre portion.

14 Arrange tomato slices in a row on the pancakes. Arrange a few paper thin slices of mushrooms on the tomatoes. Sprinkle mozzarella cheese.

15 At serving time, bake in a preheated oven at 160°C/300°F for 12-15 minutes. Garnish with parsley or mint sprigs and serve hot.

Crispy Vegetables

Crisp batter fried vegetables, stir fried in sauces at the time of serving. This dish can be eaten as a snack or can be served with a curry as a side dish.

Picture on facing page   *Serves 6-8*

INGREDIENTS

50 gm/2 oz Sugam Paneer - cut into
½" square pieces
½ of a cauliflower or broccoli - cut into
1" florets
2-3 large mushrooms - cut each piece into
2 from the middle
6 babycorns - keep whole
½ red, ½ yellow capsicum, ½ green capsicum -
cut into 1" square pieces
1 onion - cut into 8 pieces
20 basil leaves - keep whole, remove stem
1 tsp garlic paste

BATTER
¼ cup rice flour or ¼ cup raw rice (kachcha
chaawal) - ground to a powder in a mixer
¾ cup cornflour
1 tbsp chopped lemon grass, 1 tsp soya sauce
¾ cup chilled water- approx.
1 tbsp oil, ½ tsp red chilli flakes, ¾ tsp salt

MANGO CHUTNEY PASTE
1 tbsp lemon juice, 1 tbsp oil
4 dry, red chillies, 1 tbsp black bean sauce
3 tbsp ready-made mango chutney
1 tsp soya sauce, 1" stick cinnamon (dalchini)
1 tbsp tomato ketchup
1 tsp honey, ½ tsp salt

METHOD

1 Cut all vegetables as written above.

2 Put all ingredients written under mango chutney paste in a mixer and grind to a paste.

3 Use ready-made rice flour or roughly grind ½ cup rice in a mixer to a powder. Roast this ground rice in a kadhai till it starts to change colour. Sieve the roasted rice to get ¼ cup powder.

4   Mix all ingredients of batter in a bowl. Mix well and add cauliflower, baby corns, Sugam Paneer and mushrooms to the batter and keep aside for 30 minutes or more.

7   Add the mango chutney paste. Stir fry for 2 minutes.

5   Heat oil in a kadhai. Mix the vegetables in the batter well and deep fry till golden brown.

8   Add ¼ cup water.

6   At serving time, heat 1 tbsp oil add 1 tsp garlic paste and onions. Stir fry for 2 minutes. Add the capsicums. Stir.

9   Add fried vegetables and basil, mix well and serve hot.

Rice & Beans Baked in Sauce

Picture on facing page   *Serves 6*

INGREDIENTS

VEGETABLE LAYER
125 gm/4 oz Sugam Paneer - cut into ¼" pieces
200 gm/6 oz (½ of a medium) cauliflower
150 gm/5 oz (1 small flower) broccoli
2 thin carrots - very thinly sliced diagonally
juice of ½ lemon
3-4 flakes garlic - crushed
1 onion - cut into half and then into rings
¼ tsp salt
¼ tsp peppercorns (saboot kali mirch) - crushed
2 tbsp grated cheese, preferably cheddar

RICE LAYER
2 cups boiled rice
a few drops of food colour or use haldi for
boiling
2 tbsp chopped coriander, 1 tsp lemon juice
½ tsp salt and ½ tsp pepper

BEAN LAYER (MIX TOGETHER)
1 tin baked beans- use about ¾ cup
1-2 tsp tabasco sauce
salt and pepper to taste

MUSTARD SAUCE
4 tbsp plain flour (maida), 3 cups milk
2 tbsp grated cheese, preferably cheddar
¾ tsp salt and ¼ tsp pepper, or to taste
1-2 tbsp mustard sauce, or to taste
some oregano to sprinkle on top

2   Heat 2 tbsp butter. Add garlic and onions. Cook till onions turn soft. Add vegetables. Add ½ tsp salt and ¼ tsp pepper. Saute, till the vegetables gets crisp tender. Keep aside.

3   Separately mix all ingredients of the rice layer gently & keep aside 2-3 tbsp of rice for topping. Spread the remaining rice in a very thin layer in a greased dish.

METHOD

1   Cut cauliflower and broccoli into very small florets with small stalks.

4 Add Sugam Paneer to the bean mixture. Sprinkle beans and Sugam Paneer over the rice.

6 For sauce, heat 3 tbsp olive oil or butter in a pan. Add flour. Cook on slow heat for 1-2 minutes. Add milk gradually, stirring continuously. Stir till it boils. Cook for 2-3 minutes till thick of a coating consistency. Add salt, pepper and mustard. Remove from heat. Add 2 tbsp cheese.

5 Spread veggies over beans. Sprinkle 2 tbsp cheese on the vegetables. Keep aside.

7 Spread the mustard sauce over the vegetables. Sprinkle the remaining rice. Sprinkle some oregano. Bake at 200°C/ 475°F for 20 minutes till light golden or grill for 15 minutes (250°). Serve.

Cannelloni with Two Sauces

Picture on facing page   *Serves 4*

INGREDIENTS

CANNELLONI TUBES
8 ready made cannelloni tubes
1 tbsp oil and 1 tsp salt to cook the pasta
50 gm/2 oz mozzarella cheese - grated

SPINACH FILLING
2 tbsp butter, 2 flakes garlic - crushed
1 onion - finely chopped
4 cups finely shredded spinach
200 gm/6 oz diced Sugam Paneer
2 tbsp grated mozzarella cheese, 2 tbsp cream
½ tsp salt and ½ tsp pepper, or to taste

TOMATO SAUCE
2 tbsp oil, 1 onion - very finely chopped
3-4 flakes garlic - crushed
200 gm/6 oz tomato puree
½ tsp dried oregano, 1 tsp salt & ½ tsp pepper
1 tsp sugar, or to taste, 4 tbsp fresh cream

BECHAMEL SAUCE
2 tbsp butter, 2 tbsp plain flour (maida)
2 cups milk, 2 tbsp cream, salt & pepper to taste

METHOD

1 Boil ready made cannelloni tubes in boiling water with 1 tsp salt and oil for 7-8 minutes till done. Remove on greased aluminium foil. Keep the tubes separate, see that they do not overlap.

2 To prepare the Sugam Paneer-spinach filling, heat butter in a pan. Add garlic and onion and cook till transparent. Add finely shredded spinach and cook for 3-4 minutes. Add Sugam Paneer and mix well. Reduce heat and add cream, stirring continuously. Add salt and pepper to taste. Cook for a minute. Remove from heat. Add cheese. Keep aside.

3 To prepare the tomato sauce, heat oil. Add garlic. When it turns golden, add the onions and cook till light brown. Add the tomato puree and oregano. Cook on medium heat till puree turns a little dry. Add salt and pepper to taste. Reduce heat and add cream, stirring constantly till well mixed. Remove from heat.

4 To prepare the bechamel sauce, heat butter. Add maida and stir for ½ minute. Reduce heat and add milk, stirring continuously. Cook stirring till it starts to coat the spoon. Reduce heat, add cream, stirring well to mix. Add salt and pepper to taste and remove from heat.

5 Stuff the boiled tubes with spinach-Sugam Paneer mixture.

6 To assemble, spread some tomato sauce at the base of the dish.

7 Arrange the stuffed tubes on it in a row.

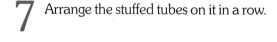

8 Spoon the left over tomato sauce on the top. Then cover the tomato sauce with bechamel sauce.

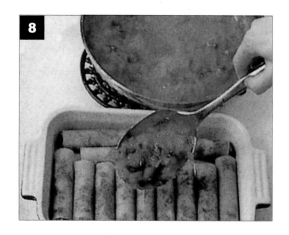

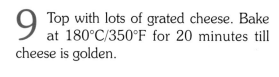

9 Top with lots of grated cheese. Bake at 180°C/350°F for 20 minutes till cheese is golden.

HINDI OR ENGLISH NAMES USED IN INDIA	ENGLISH NAMES AS USED IN USA/UK/ OTHER COUNTRIES
Aloo	Potatoes
Amchoor (Mango Powder)	Raw mangoes are sun dried and ground to a fine powder. It is used as a souring agent instead of lime or lemon juice in cooked dishes.
Badaam	Almonds
Baingan	Eggplant, aubergine
Basmati rice	Fragrant Indian rice
Bhutta	Corn
Bhindi	Okra, Lady finger
Black Bean Sauce	Made from fermented black beans. It is slightly thicker than soya sauce and has a sweeter taste than soya sauce. Available ready-made in bottles.
Black Salt	It is also called rock salt. It is pinkish in colour and different in flavour than the regular salt. Used as an important ingredient in certain spice blends.
Capsicum	Bell peppers
Chaawal, Chawal	Rice
Chana	Chickpeas
Chana Dal	Yellow split peas
Chhoti Illaichi	Green cardamom
Chilli powder	Red chilli powder, Cayenne pepper
Cornflour	Cornstarch
Cream	Whipping cream
Dalchini	Cinnamon
Degi Mirch	Kashmiri red chillies ground to a powder. Degi mirch imparts a bright red colour to the curry without making it hot.

Dhaniya Powder (Coriander Seeds, Ground) — Coriander seeds are ground to a fine powder. This is an important constituent of most curries. It helps in thickening curries.

French beans — Green beans

Gajar — Carrots

Gobhi — Cauliflower

Hara Dhania — Cilantro/fresh or green coriander

Hari Gobhi — Broccoli

Hari Mirch — Green hot peppers, green chillies, serrano peppers

Illaichi — Cardamom

Imli — Tamarind

Javitri (Mace) — This is the lacy covering of the seed of the nutmeg tree. It has a rich, warm fragrance and a sweet flavour. Use it very sparingly, adding it to only rich and creamy dishes. Mostly it is added to various spice blends.

Jaiphal (Nutmeg) — It is the oval, brown kernel of the seed of the nutmeg tree. It has a rich warm fragrance and a sweet antiseptic flavour. It is generally grated and just a pinch is added to dishes.

Jeera Powder — Ground cumin seeds

Kaju — Cashewnuts

Kari patta (Curry Leaves) — They are available fresh or dried. Most Indian homes grow a young plant in a pot, so as to get maximum flavour from the fresh leaves. Used abundantly in South-Indian cooking.

Katori — Individual serving bowls resembling ramekins

Khumb — Mushrooms

Kishmish — Raisins

Kofta — Balls made from minced vegetables or meat, fried and put in a curry/gravy/sauce.

Maida — White flour

Makai, Makki — Corn

Makhan — Butter

Matar — Peas

Mitha soda — Baking soda

Nimbu — Lemon

Patta Gobhi — Cabbage

Phalli		Green beans
Powdered sugar		Castor sugar
Pyaz, pyaaz		Onions
Rai, Sarson (Mustard Seeds)		These may be small reddish brown (rai) or slighter bigger blackish (sarson) seeds. They have a sharp, pungent flavour which mellows after they are cooked in hot oil or dry roasted. The Southern part of India uses mustard to flavour almost all their dishes.
Red Capsicum		Red bell peppers
Red chilli flakes		Red pepper flakes
Saboot Kali mirch		Peppercorns
Saunf		Fennel
Sela Chaawal		Parboiled rice, which when cooked is not sticky at all
Seviyaan		Vermicelli
Shimla Mirch		Green bell peppers
Soda bicarb		Baking soda
Spring Onions		Green onions, Scallions
Suji		Semolina
Tamatar		Tomato
Til		Sesame seeds
Yellow Capsicum		Yellow bell peppers
Jeera		Cumin seeds

The Indian Spice Box

Mostly every Indian kitchen will have this box with various compartments to hold the basic spices & salt.

Dhania Powder Jeera
Salt Haldi
Amchoor Red Chilli Powder
Garam Masala

Indian Spice Blends

Which perk up the flavour of Indian dishes.

GARAM MASALA

Makes ¼ cup

5-6 2" sticks cinnamon (dalchini)
15-20 black cardamom pods (moti illaichi)
¾ tbsp cloves (laung)
2 tbsp black peppercorns (saboot kali mirch)
2 tbsp cumin seeds (jeera)
½ flower of mace (javitri)

1. Remove seeds of black cardamoms. Discard skin.
2. Roast all ingredients together in a skillet for 2 minutes on low heat, stirring constantly, till fragrant.
3. Remove from heat. Cool. Grind to a fine powder in a clean coffee or spice grinder. Store in a small jar with a tight fitting lid.

CHAT MASALA

Makes 3/4 cup

3 tbsp cumin seeds (jeera)
1 tbsp ground ginger (sonth)
2 tsp carom seeds (ajwain)
2 tsp raw mango powder (amchoor)
2 tbsp ground, black salt (kala namak)
1 tsp salt, 1 tsp ground black pepper
½ tsp ground nutmeg (jaiphal)

1. Roast cumin seeds in a small nonstick skillet or a wok to a golden brown colour. Transfer to a bowl and set aside.
2. Roast carom seeds over moderate heat for about 2 minutes, till fragrant.
3. Grind roasted cumin seeds and carom seeds. Mix in the remaining ingredients.
4. Store in an air tight jar.

TANDOORI MASALA

Makes ½ cup

2 tbsp coriander seeds (saboot dhania)
2 tbsp cumin seeds (jeera)
1 tsp fenugreek seeds (methi daana)
1 tbsp black peppercorns (saboot kali mirch)
1 tbsp cloves (laung)
seeds of 8 black cardamom pods (moti illaichi)
2 tsp paprika (degi mirch)
1 tbsp dried fenugreek leaves (kasoori methi)
1 tbsp ground cinnamon (dalchini)
½ tbsp ground ginger (sonth)
½ tsp red chilli powder

1. In a nonstick skillet, roast together — coriander seeds, cumin seeds, fenugreek seeds, black pepper corns, cloves and cardamom seeds, on moderate heat for about 1 minute, until fragrant.
2. Remove from heat and let the spices cool down. Grind to a fine powder. Transfer to a bowl and mix in the remaining ingredients. Store in an air tight jar.

Some Cooking Utensils

KADHAI (wok) - The kadhai is a deep pan, round bottomed with two handles on the sides. Used mainly for frying and making Indian masala dishes. When buying one, choose a heavy bottomed one and of a medium size. Steel/Brass kadhais were used earlier, but now aluminium or non stick ones are more popular. Copper bottomed metal kadhais are also becoming popular.

TAWA (griddle) - A heavy iron tawa makes good chappatis. Buy one with a handle. These days non stick griddles are also available.

Sauce Pan - These are deep pans with a handle. Useful for making tea, blanching vegetables in water or working with food where some sauce is needed. Usually these are made of stainless steel and are available in various sizes. Nonstick ones are also available.

PATILA (deep metal pans) - Used for boiling water, milk, rice, pasta etc. Buy a heavy bottom one. Deep non stick pots with handles are also available which are very handy for making soups, rice and curries.

NON STICK FRYING PAN (saute pan, skillet) -

A pan about 2" high is ideal for shallow frying tikkis, kebabs and other snacks. It makes a good utensil for cooking dry/semi dry dishes too. The vegetables lie flat in a single layer on the wide bottom making them crunchy on the outside and yet moist from inside. Remember to use a plastic or a wooden spoon/spatula to stir and fry in all nonstick vessels. Metallic ones will scratch the non stick finish and ruin it. Avoid strong detergents for washing them, warm soapy water is best. It is good to have one small (about 7" diameter) and one big (10 " diameter) pan. Dosas and pancakes too can be made conveniently in them.

KADCCHI (laddle) -

Large, long handled spoon with a small shallow bowl like spoon at the end. Should be strong enough for stirring masalas.

PALTA (pancake turner) -

These broad metal turners have thin, flexible yet sturdy blade that will slide easily under the food and then be strong enough to turn the food. Not just for pancakes, it's great for turning kebabs too. Ideally choose one with a heat resistant handle.

CHAKLA-BELAN (rolling board-rolling pin) -

A marble or heavy weight rolling board is ideal for rolling out dough for chapattis, poori etc. A wooden rolling pin with it makes the set complete. Plastic rolling pins are available but I am not too comfortable with them.

PARAT (shallow bowl to knead dough) -

Shallow bowl to make dough, generally stainless steel. Buy a medium size even if you are a small family, because if the bowl is too small, the surrounding area tends to get messy while making the dough. Dough can also be made in a food processor.

STEEL KI BIG CHHANNI (colander)

A big, wide strainer with large holes for draining cooked rice, pasta and for draining fresh vegetables after washing.

CHHARA, PAUNI (slotted spoon)

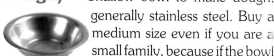

A big round, flat spoon with holes and a long handle. Serves good for removing fried food from oil as it drains out the oil nicely through the holes. Also used to lift solid foods out of cooking liquids.